THE JUVENILE LIBRARY

General Editor

Brian W. Alderson

VICTOR E. NEUBURG

———

The Penny Histories

———

'When Guy, Earl of Warwick, and Parismus
and Parismenus, and Valentine and Orson, and
the Seven Champions of England, were handed
round at school—were they not all purchased
with my pocket-money?'   Uncle Toby
          (*Tristram Shandy,* Book VI, Chapter 32)

VICTOR E. NEUBURG

The Penny Histories

A study of chapbooks for young readers over two centuries

Illustrated with facsimiles of seven chapbooks

London

OXFORD UNIVERSITY PRESS

1968

Oxford University Press, Ely House, London W.1

GLASGOW NEW YORK TORONTO MELBOURNE WELLINGTON
CAPE TOWN SALISBURY IBADAN NAIROBI LUSAKA ADDIS ABABA
BOMBAY CALCUTTA MADRAS KARACHI LAHORE DACCA
KUALA LUMPUR HONG KONG TOKYO

Printed by Fletcher & Son Ltd., Norwich

Acknowledgements

Among the many debts incurred in the writing of this book, those which I acknowledge with the deepest sense of pleasure and obligation are to my wife and daughter for their continued encouragement; and to Barbara Gilbert for reading the first draft critically, and typing a later one impeccably.

V.E.N.

Sources: The facsimiles of *Guy, Earl of Warwick, Fairy Stories, The Children in the Wood,* and *Cock Robin* have been made from copies in the British Museum; *A Peep at Various Nations* has been made from a copy in the New York Public Library, *Toads and Diamonds* from a copy in the John Johnson collection at Oxford, and *The Rod* from a copy in the possession of the author.

The woodcuts on the cover and on pages 19, 33, 45, 77, and 220 are reproduced from nineteenth-century broadsides and other material in the British Museum collection of *York publications by J. Kendrew*. The title-page on page 54 is taken from an illustration in the Rosenbach catalogue of *Early American children's books*, other illustrations are from chapbooks in the British Museum (pp. 14, 25, 39, 60–61), the Johnson collection (p. 63) and in the possession of the author (p. 76).

Contents

'The old classics of the nursery'

One morning early in July, 1763, James Boswell visited the printing office in Bow Churchyard which was run by the Dicey family. There he bought a number of chapbooks which, he said, had amused him in his childhood. 'I have always retained a kind of affection for them, as they recall my early days,' he wrote on the flyleaf of a bound volume of his chapbooks which now forms part of the Child Memorial Collection in Harvard College Library.

Other eighteenth-century writers had looked back with pleasure upon these little books which Lamb described as 'the old classics of the nursery'; and Wordsworth, Coleridge and Crabbe have all mentioned reading them in their early days, while Samuel Bamford described how every farthing he could scrape together was spent in purchasing *Jack the Giant-Killer*, *Saint George and the Dragon*, *Tom Hickathrift* and *The Seven Champions of Christendom*. Much earlier in the century, too—in *The Tatler* in 1709—Sir Richard Steele had described his small godson as an authority upon chapbook heroes like Guy of Warwick.

At a period when children's books were overtly moral and didactic in tone[1], it was hardly surprising that juvenile readers should turn eagerly to these small, not unattractive little books which formed almost the entire reading matter of the poorer classes in eighteenth-century England. In them were to be found abridged versions of the romances of knights and maidens which had delighted medieval audiences; tales of giants, monsters and fairies, many of which represented the residue of an oral lore whose origins were rooted in a long-lost antiquity; songs and jests, stories of pirates and highwaymen. Little wonder that young readers found chapbooks more exciting than the more seriously intentioned books which they were offered[2].

[1] See W. Sloane, *Children's Books in England and America in the Seventeenth Century*, New York, King's Crown Press, Columbia University, 1955.

[2] 'Some,' wrote Francis Fox (*circa* 1754), 'are of the opinion, that children would sooner come to read English well, if they were not constantly kept to read the Bible, but were sometimes put to read other books. . . .' Fox's suggestions, however, hardly seem likely to have achieved his aim. They include Ostervald's *Abridgment of the History of the Bible*, price 1d.; *Pastoral Advice Before Confirmation*, price 2d.; and *Dr. Woodward Against Profane Language*, price 1d.

Chapbooks, or 'penny histories' as they were sometimes called, formed the most important and numerically the most considerable element in the printed popular literature of the eighteenth century, and although they attracted the attention of book-collectors like George Daniel, the celebrated Richard Heber, Thomas Gaisford, E. V. Utterson and J. O. Halliwell in the nineteenth century, they have remained comparatively unnoticed in the twentieth. Contemporary bibliographical techniques have not yet been fully employed to investigate the extent of chapbook literature, its production and distribution, and above all its social significance in terms of the growth of literacy and the development of children's literature.

The derivation of the word 'chapbook' is uncertain; it may have been a corruption of the word 'cheap', or it may have derived from the Old English 'ceap' (trade). It is very much easier to define chapbooks than to establish with any certainty whence the word came: chapbooks were the paper-covered books offered for sale by pedlars, hawkers and other itinerant merchants who were generally known as chapmen. During the centuries when there were few shops outside the towns, the chapman was an essential link in the distribution to isolated village communities and farms of such articles as pins, needles, ribbons, thread, and the many other small items which would be required from time to time in every household. From the closing years of the seventeenth century an important part of his stock-in-trade was a bundle of small books which he sold at the cost of a copper or two.

The emergence of the chapbook at this point, in succession to the black-letter broadside ballad, was noted by the late Cyprian Blagden: '. . . people turned against Black Letter at the end of the seventeenth century. . . . There was, of course, no nice clean ending; it guttered out in the stronger light of the eighteenth-century chapbook and the purely topical ballad.' To record a shift in popular taste, however, is not to explain it. Robert Southey, whose well-known telling of the *Three Little Bears* is remembered without his authorship, and whose tremendous output of prose and verse is largely forgotten, wrote: 'The Public and Transubstantiation I hold to be the two greatest mysteries in or out of nature'; and any attempt to analyse the further mystery of the

Public's changing taste must lie outside the scope of the present study. It is probable, however, that the proliferation of pamphlet literature during the Civil War and during Commonwealth days had given ordinary men a taste for something more substantial in form than a single sheet with a ballad printed on it; and an even more fruitful line of inquiry would be into the nature of the chapbook as one manifestation of the growing interest in books, with the consequent spread of literacy amongst all sections of society, including the poorest classes.

Whatever the cause, the chapbook was well established at the beginning of the eighteenth century. Religious tracts constituted the only other really inexpensive reading matter of the day; chapbooks represented a secular strand in popular culture, and offered a striking contrast to those cheap religious publications which the Society for Promoting Christian Knowledge had begun issuing for mass distribution very soon after its foundation in 1699. Chapbooks circulated in their thousands during the eighteenth century. They were the successors of the Elizabethan jest-books, which were fewer in number and enjoyed a very much more restricted circulation. The Commonwealth period witnessed the suppression of these merriments, and the contentious religious and political tracts which took their place fed upon a public appetite for controversy which waned towards the close of the seventeenth century.

In physical appearance chapbooks were not unpleasing. The woodcut illustrations possessed a vitality which outweighed the undoubted crudity of their execution, and the variety of types used upon the title-pages was appealing to the eye and must have caught the attention of the contemporary purchaser whose lack of sophistication in matters of typography was matched by a sense of the permanence and authority of the printed word[1].

Chapbooks usually measured about six inches by four inches (though in the nineteenth century they were often much smaller), and generally, though not always, consisted of twenty-four pages. They were issued unbound, and the title-page referred to above also did duty as a wrapper, nearly always with a woodcut illustration. The

[1] Cf. Willa Muir, *Living with Ballads*, London, 1965, p. 232.

coarse rag-paper used in the production of chapbooks did little to enhance their physical appearance, and it is a remarkable tribute to the Diceys and other chapbook printers of the eighteenth century that their wares possessed a visual charm and individuality which has survived for over two hundred years.

Very few chapbooks contained original material, and those which did were invariably of some immediately topical interest. The unknown authors of these little books drew upon a number of printed and traditional sources, and in an age when copyright had little force, not only were the contents of a chapbook copied by one printer from another, but sometimes the illustrations were faithfully imitated as well!

One of the most important sources from which chapbooks drew their contents was that of medieval romance. Tales of antiquity had become part of the traditional lore of the English people, and continued to be read by the poorer classes up to the period of the Romantic Revival. Such romances, as Sir Walter Scott pointed out, 'fell into disrepute, though some of the more popular, sadly abridged and adulterated, continued to

7

be published in chapbooks as they are called'. The survival of these examples of medieval literature is an example of the way in which such themes laid hold upon the popular imagination and have persisted in one form or another right down to our own day. In their original versions they appealed to a literate and sophisticated medieval audience, and as they declined they became not only the stuff of romantic fiction for the common people of eighteenth-century England—amongst whom lingered lively remains of a medieval culture from which such romances had originally sprung—but also the earliest books for children which provided the qualities of wholesomeness and excitement which have always been amongst the most important and enduring features of juvenile fiction.

The most typical of these romances is *Guy of Warwick*, which was known in the thirteenth century. In its printed form, the first edition was probably that issued by Richard Pynson some time before 1500. The account of Guy's adventures that it contained must have long been familiar to the public, since it closely resembled a fourteenth-century version of the legend which was extremely popular. Numerous printed editions followed Pynson's. Wynkyn de Worde, William Copland and John Cawood printed it, and Copland's version had woodcut illustrations; John Paston's inventory of books, made around 1480, showed two romances dealing with Guy of Warwick; and Shakespeare, Skelton, Drayton and other writers were almost certainly familiar with it. In 1579 the romance is described as being by a writer who is 'both witty and pleasant'; and there seems no reason at all to doubt the extreme popularity of this work, despite the strictures of the Puritan, Edward Dering, who in 1572 described it as being a book of 'childish follye'.

The fiction of the Middle Ages continued to be enjoyed by a large and apparently growing circle of readers, and in 1592 *Guy of Warwick* appeared as a ballad printed on a single sheet. It was constantly reprinted and had a tremendous vogue. Before the close of the sixteenth century, however, the cultivated public had turned away from the old romances in favour of the *novelle* of Renaissance Italy, and from about the middle of the seventeenth century, admirers of *Guy of Warwick* were to be found chiefly amongst

9

less sophisticated readers[1]; and when chap-books began to appear at the close of the seventeenth century, numerous editions of Guy's exploits were published in this way.

The survival of medieval romance in chap-book form meant principally that the language of the story changed very consider-ably. The short couplets in which the four-teenth-century version had been composed, and the somewhat wearisome metrical ver-sions which succeeded it, gave way to the crude and occasionally vigorous prose which characterized some of the better chapbook editions of the old romances. Besides a re-telling of the story, the chapbook provided an abridgement which was very much more suitable for reading than the often prolix verse which had delighted generations of listeners in the Middle Ages. The following

[1] For a valuable discussion of this important issue I am indebted to R. S. Crane, *The Vogue of 'Guy of Warwick' from the close of the Middle Ages to the Romantic Revival.* (Publications of The Modern Language Association of America, Vol. XXX, 2, 1915), p. 167, note 7. He mentions three reasons for this: (i) there is no evidence that seven-teenth-century men of letters were interested in medieval romance; (ii) surviving stories were published entirely by printers engaged in the ballad and later, the chapbook trade; (iii) in plays and other literary works of the time a taste for the old romances is treated as a characteristic of old women, servants and children.

lines, which conclude an early version of *Guy of Warwick*, will, if compared with the closing lines of the facsimile, show the tremendous differences which existed between the renderings of this once most popular story:

'Now is the story brought to an end,
Of Guy, the bold baron of price,
And of the fair maid Felice,
And of Aslake, and Sir Raynbron.
Fair ensamples man may lere,
Whoso will listen and hear,
True to love, late and early,
As, in his life, did good Sir Guy:
For he forsook worldly honour,
To serve God, his creatour;
Wherefore Jesu, that was of a maid born
To buy man's soul that was forlorn,
And rose from death the third day,
And led man's soul from hell away,
On their souls have mercy!
And ye, that have heard this story,
God give you all his blessing,
And of his grace to your ending;
And joy, and bliss, that ever shall be!
Amen, Amen, for charité!'

(From George Ellis: *Specimens of early English Metrical Romances,* p. 238.)

Guy of Warwick, of course, was not the only medieval romance to survive as a chapbook. As Lord Ernle has pointed out:

'. . . . Two centuries later [i.e. from 1597], in the debased form of chap-books, knights-errant still roamed the country among the laces and ribbons of the pedlar's pack . . . the medieval romances were the pioneers of popular literature.'[1]

Romances which were reprinted as chap-books included *Bevis of Southampton, The Four Sons of Aymon, The Seven Wise Masters*; and while none of these enjoyed the popularity of the knight of Warwick, they were none the less often reprinted as penny histories throughout the eighteenth century.

The story of Faust was a popular chap-book, and was one of several constantly reprinted titles which came from Germany. The many-sided fascination of the Faust theme ensured its popularity, and as a story of magic it could hardly have failed to appeal to children. *Fortunatus*, first published in Augsburg in 1509, had many German suc-

[1] *The Light Reading of our Ancestors*, London, 1927, p. 107.

cessors, and first appeared in England in 1600. Dekker adapted it as a play, and the story was long reprinted as a chapbook. So, too, was the legend of *The Wandering Jew*, which was first known in England from a German version, its origins being unknown. Another popular title, *The Famous History of Valentine and Orson*, was originally French; and indeed borrowings from continental sources represented quite a considerable element in chapbook literature.

While a detailed analysis of the precise extent to which chapbook literature was indebted to French, German and even Italian sources lies outside the present writer's terms of reference, the enduring popularity of continental tales must be stressed. The title-pages of the two editions of *Valentine and Orson* on pp. 14 and 61 indicate the popularity of a French romance that lasted for well over one hundred years as an English chapbook, and it would be an interesting and perhaps not too jingoistic task to trace how far most of these foreign heroes became increasingly anglicized as time went on. The exceptions were characters like Faust, who retained an aura of mystery which seemed essential for plots dealing in magic, the Devil and the

THE
HISTORY
OF
Valentine and *Orson.*

Reader, you'll find this little Book contains
Enough to answer thy Expence and Pains;
And if with Caution you will read it thro',
'Twill both Instruct thee and Delight thee
too.

Printed and sold in Aldermary Church-Yard
Bow-Lane, London.

supernatural which were traditionally set in 'high Germany'.

English legend and folklore was equally important. In chapbooks like *Nixon's Cheshire Prophecy*, *Mother Shipton's Prophecy* or *Mother Bunch's Golden Fortune Teller*, we see a great deal of traditional material which would have been familiar to most English people in a pre-industrial society. The folklore sources of English chapbooks have never been examined, and it is certain that the results of such an investigation would shed a great deal of light upon the survival of age-old beliefs amongst the urban and rural poor in eighteenth-century England, and upon their social *mores*.

More important from the point of view of young readers was the fact that fairy tales were available to them only in chapbook form. The rich tradition of English fairy mythology survived in the eighteenth century almost entirely because of chapbooks. Like the medieval romances, fairy legends and tales had remained popular amongst educated people until about the middle of the seventeenth century, and they declined similarly round about this time. Through chapbooks, children had immediate and ready access to a very considerable range of traditional literature that their more sophisticated elders had, for better or worse, outgrown. It should be stressed that romances and fairy tales at this period were only available as chapbooks, and without them eighteenth-century children would have been deprived of works which not only enriched their imagination but also provided opportunities for wonder and delight[1].

Other material used by chapbook authors was drawn from Elizabethan jest-books and ballad sheets; less often from items of local lore; and sometimes from popular authors like Thomas Deloney or Daniel Defoe. The overwhelming impression gained from a study of eighteenth-century chapbooks is that of an extraordinary variety in their contents. In addition to the fiction already described, there were household manuals, collections of ballads, and a good deal of sensational literature which today would find its way into the columns of the more popular newspapers. Some of these chapbooks may well have

[1] Cf. Wordsworth (*The Prelude*, V, ll. 341–344)

> 'Oh! give us once again the Wishing-Cap
> Of Fortunatus, and the invisible Coat
> Of Jack the Giant-killer, Robin Hood,
> And Sabra in the forest with St. George!'

found their way into the hands of children; but undoubtedly the romances and fairy tales would have made the greatest appeal to them, and it was these chapbooks which were printed in the greatest numbers.

The fairy tales published in a chapbook by Dicey, reproduced on pp. 105–128, form one of the earliest collections of fairy legends to have been printed in a popular form. It appeared at a time when traces of the traditional oral lore of faery still survived amongst the English peasantry. By the end of the eighteenth century it had declined considerably, and the fairy stories which had once laid so great a hold upon the imagination of men and women in a pre-literate society became—largely because of their survival in chapbooks—an important element in children's literature; and this they have remained ever since, with no apparent diminution in their popularity.

A number of chapbook heroes remain still very much a part of a living tradition, either in nursery rhymes or in the fairy tales which have a perennial appeal. 'Perhaps,' wrote George Orwell, 'the basic myth of the Western World is Jack the Giant-Killer'; and heroes of this type abound in chapbooks. There seem to have been two kinds of archetypal figure, one the 'serious' hero like Robin Hood, Jack the Giant-Killer, Guy of Warwick, Tom Thumb or Fortunatus, and the other a comic hero of whom Simple Simon—whose adventures were often recounted in chapbooks—is the supreme example. The appeal of both types of hero is universal; the serious and the comic hero both seem to satisfy a fundamental need on the part of the audience, and this is no less true today than it was in the past. Few characters of children's fiction today are better known than Billy Bunter, who is a direct descendant of the comic hero of this fugitive literature of more than two centuries ago; and the same is true of Sherlock Holmes, the 'serious' hero whose name is a household word.

As we have seen, the penny histories were intended for adults, but they were read by young readers in the absence of children's books other than those which had a strongly doctrinal or theological bias. Occasionally voices were raised against chapbooks. In 1702 Thomas White cautioned his young readers in a school-book entitled *A Little Book for Little Children*[1]: 'When thou canst read, read

[1] Apparently a very popular manual; the edition of 1702 was the twelfth.

no Ballads and foolish Books, but the Bible.'
This sentiment was echoed many years later
in a textbook published in America in 1770:

'Hate vulgar impious songs, a wretched chime,
Where fulsome nonsense jingles into rhyme.'

Yet another, somewhat longer, attack upon
chapbooks had appeared in the anonymous
The History of Genesis, published in 1708:

'It is indeed a great Blessing of God, that
Children in England have liberty to read the
holy Scriptures, when others abroad are denied
it. And yet alas! how often do we see Parents
prefer "Tom Thumb," "Guy of Warwick", or

some such foolish Book, before the Book of Life! Let not your Children read these vain Books, profane Ballads, and filthy songs. Throw away all fond and amorous Romances, and fabulous Histories of Giants, the bombast Atchievements of Knight Errantry, and the like; for these fill the Heads of Children with vain, silly and idle imaginations.'

In spite of such exhortations, these small books must have had a very considerable attraction for children, and there seems no reason to doubt that they were widely read by young people at a time when alternative literature seemed dull in comparison with the magic world of giants, heroes and fairies which was within such easy reach in the pages of the penny histories.

2

Bow Churchyard and the running stationers

A comprehensive survey of the chapbook trade in the eighteenth and nineteenth centuries would be a very considerable undertaking, and it is unlikely that completeness could ever be achieved. In London alone, over two centuries, about two hundred and fifty firms and individuals were concerned in their production and there were numerous others in all the larger provincial towns, and in some of the smaller ones as well.

There is a further complication in the fact that the distinction between printer, publisher and bookseller is often so blurred as to be virtually non-existent. On the other hand, sufficient chapbooks are preserved in the British Museum, the Bodleian Library, Harvard College Library and other institutions, to make the task of reconstructing a reasonable outline of the chapbook trade possible.

Few chapbooks were dated, but most—though by no means all—did indicate on their title-page the name of a printer or publisher[1], and our understanding of chapbook literature is facilitated by this fact. The almost complete destruction of records regarding production and distribution makes precision impossible, but from a close study of chapbook imprints a great deal of information can be gained. The adaptation of modern photographic processes for studying paper and for cataloguing variations in woodcut pictures and ornaments may also yield some information which could be used in assigning and dating early chapbooks.

The earliest chapbook printers were Thomas Norris, William Onley, G. Sawbridge, Philip Brooksby, Josiah Blare, Joshua Conyers and William Thackeray. All these men had been active in the ballad trade at the close of the seventeenth century, and when the public turned against black-letter, they printed and sold large numbers of chapbooks; but facts concerning them are scanty. Onley makes a brief appearance in John Dunton's *Life and Errors* (1705), while Norris

[1] Those whose imprint is simply 'Licensed and Entered According to Order', 'Printed in the Present Year', or 'Printed and Sold in London', etc., offer no clue as to who produced them, and present the bibliographer with a cluster of insoluble problems.

is known to have been a churchwarden of St. Magnus Church on London Bridge, and was described by a contemporary as 'a very rich bookseller . . . whose country seat was at Holloway'; but of the others little is known save their addresses. These changed surprisingly little during the eighteenth century, when the printing of chapbooks was centred upon London Bridge, Bow Churchyard, and Little Britain and Pye Corner which were both near to Smithfield.

Thomas Norris was at *The Looking Glass* on London Bridge, and was probably succeeded there by James Hodges, a printer and publisher who ran a considerable business. Hodges was elected Town Clerk of the City of London, and in 1758 he was knighted by George II. One of his apprentices, Stanley Crowder, succeeded his master at *The Looking Glass*, and later moved to *The Golden Ball* in Paternoster Row. Here he was associated with Henry Woodgate, an unsuccessful publisher and bookseller who went bankrupt in 1766. Woodgate was also in partnership with Samuel Brooks, during the course of which they published no less than one hundred and forty-three chapbooks.

It will be seen that the earliest members of

the book trade concerned with ephemeral literature formed a small and fairly tightly-knit group, and it is hard to resist the conclusion that the chapbook trade was shared between them. Their premises were close together, and the market was sufficiently large and buoyant to permit of such co-operation.

The procedures followed in the printing offices remain a matter for surmise. While chapbooks formed a not inconsiderable part of the stock-in-trade of several eighteenth-century printers, it does not appear that any great care was taken in their production, though later printers like Kendrew, Rusher and Catnach set a higher standard. The texts of the earliest chapbooks were taken from indefinite sources—a ballad sheet, perhaps, from which the verses had to be turned into prose; a mutilated Elizabethan jest-book, printed in black-letter; or even an oral version of some traditional tale which was recalled by the printer or his assistant. The necessity of fitting a story into a certain number of pages often created difficulties, which were solved either by cutting the text or by the use of woodcut illustrations. A space at the end of a chapbook was usually filled with a list of other penny histories

To RUSHER's fam'd Warehouse,
Good children repair;
Books, Pictures, and Toys,
In abundance are there:

For youth of all ages
He's plenty in store;
Amusement, instruction,
For rich and for poor.

Woodcut of a printing office used in many of the
chapbooks issued by J. G. Rusher of Banbury.

issued by the printer, or sometimes an extra woodcut.

For all these early printers, publishers and booksellers, chapbooks represented only part of their activities—Norris, for example, published many nautical books—and it was left to a provincial printer, who ran printing establishments in London and Northampton simultaneously, to exploit the growing demand for popular literature, and specialize for three-quarters of a century in this aspect of printing, publishing and bookselling.

William Dicey, about whose antecedents little is known, began printing in St. Ives, Huntingdon, where he founded a local newspaper. Here he met Robert Raikes[1], and together they established *The Northampton Mercury* in 1720, and started printing chapbooks. When Raikes moved to Gloucester the partnership continued for a few years, and in 1725 the *Mercury* passed into the sole control of William Dicey.

At the printing office in Northampton, Dicey did all kinds of jobbing and bookselling, but all the time he continued the production of chapbooks. Precisely when he

[1] His son was later famous as the founder of the Sunday School movement.

began printing in London it is impossible to say, but there is some reason to believe that he visited the capital in 1713. His eldest son, Cluer, was in partnership with his father in 1732, and was probably in charge of the London branch of the business which may have been started some years before. It is quite possible that initially chapbooks were printed in Northampton and transported to London where they were sold.

By 1739 the Dicey printing and bookselling business in London was well established, and for more than half a century the Dicey family were the largest producers of chapbooks which were, they claimed, 'Printed in a neater Manner, and with better Cuts, more truly adapted to each story than elsewhere.' Their premises in Bow Churchyard became the centre of the trade, and from there they issued a stream of chapbooks and topical broadsides. The output of the Dicey printing presses was enormous; about one hundred and fifty different chapbook titles are recorded, a total which must be an understatement. In any case it does not include the broadsides and other ephemeral papers and games which made up the very considerable volume of material which came from this family business under some forty different imprints.

A large number of Dicey chapbooks has survived. They published little or no original matter, and their chapbooks covered the entire range of traditional literature. The Diceys were the first to attempt to cater for the mass market in a systematic way—pioneers in the field of cheap publishing on a large scale. Their achievement has never been fully recognized; but the pattern they set was followed by the brothers William and Robert Chambers, and by Charles Knight, William Milner and others during the nineteenth century.

Quite apart from chapbooks which would have been read by children, at least three books intended for young readers probably came from the Dicey press, although it is impossible to assign a date to them. These were: *Cock Robin, a pretty gilded Toy for either Girl or Boy, suited to children of all ages*; *The Tragical Death of A, Apple Pye, who was cut in pieces and eat by twenty-five gentlemen, with whom all little people ought to be well acquainted*[1]; and

[1] Cf. John Eachard, *Observations upon the answer to an enquiry into the grounds and occasions of the contempt of the Clergy*, 1671: 'Why not A apple-pasty, B baked it, C cut it, D divided it, E eat it, F fought for it, G got it', etc.

The House that Jack Built; a diverting story for Children of all ages; and the history of Gog and Magog. J. O. Halliwell has commented upon the rarity of such little books.

Despite the extent of their activities over a long period, very little is known about individual members of the Dicey family. William, the founder, died in 1753; and his son Cluer, who took over the business, was active until some time during the seventeen-sixties. Cluer's son Thomas was in business in Bow Churchyard in 1800; and the great-grandson of the founder, also Thomas, took his degree at Cambridge in 1811. His obituary notice in *The Northampton Mercury* refers to his father's residence, Claybrook Hall in Leicestershire, which seems an indication that the Dicey enterprises had been very successful.

About the end of the eighteenth century, when the taste for chapbooks was already on the wane, the Diceys were directing their energies towards other business activities. *The Northampton Mercury* remained in their possession for many years, and Thomas, great-grandson of the founder, was chairman for some years of the Midland Counties Railway.

The distribution of chapbooks was a

simple matter. They could be bought directly from the printer or publisher, and chapmen were able to buy them wholesale. These chapmen—'running stationers' as they were sometimes called—travelled the length and breadth of England with their wares, and thus the chapbooks they sold enjoyed a very wide circulation. John Clare, at the end of the eighteenth century, refers to 'tales that are hawked about a street for a penny', and also to saving money to buy books 'when hawkers offered them for sale at the door'.

A typical advertisement refers to the printer's premises—'Where any Country Chapmen or Others may be Furnished with all sorts of Historys, small Books, and Ballads, at Reasonable Rates.' The somewhat vague 'reasonable rates' left some scope for negotiation, and the wholesale price would most likely depend upon the quantity purchased. Francis Douce, whose splendid chapbook collection is now in the Bodleian Library, told a story about Sir Joseph Banks's sister, who was herself a collector of chapbooks. She went into a shop in Shoe Lane, selected a dozen penny books and paid one shilling for them. To her surprise, she was given threepence change and told to take two more. The bookseller was under the impression that she was a trade customer, and was offering her the usual discount on penny histories—thirteen or fourteen to the dozen for ninepence. There is a more definite guide to the wholesale prices paid for chapbooks in a catalogue issued by Cluer Dicey and Richard Marshall in 1764. In it, 'Penny History Books' are sold at one hundred and four for two shillings and sixpence, and 'Small Histories or Books of Amusement for Children, on various subjects, adorned with a Variety of Cuts, 100 at 6s., ditto stitch'd on embossed paper, 13 for 9d.' Two more expensive titles were *The Dutch Fortune Teller*, which cost thirteen shillings and sixpence per dozen, and *Robin Hood's Garlands*, with twenty-nine illustrations, was sold at sixteen shillings per hundred to the running stationers and retailed at sixpence. The difference between 'Penny Histories' and 'Small Histories' is not at all clear, and the alphabetical list of titles makes no distinction at all between them. It may have been simply a matter of the number of pages.

Of the running stationers little is known, and they have left behind them no trace of their arduous lives. Only Thomas Holcroft, whose parents were at one time pedlars in East Anglia, refers to the period of his childhood in the seventeen-fifties when he accompanied them on their travels:

'. . . we passed on to the Isle of Ely,' he wrote in his *Memoirs*, 'hawking our different wares, pins, laces, tempting ribbons, and garters, in every village we came to; arriving first at Peterborough, and afterwards taking care to be present at Wisbeach Fair. Markets, fairs, and wakes, were indeed the great objects which regulated all our motions.'[1]

The existence of itinerant merchants called into being a large number of guide-books, in which the importance of the chapmen was often stressed by the use of this term in the title. As early as 1687 the *City and Country Chapman's Almanack* had appeared. *The Chapman's and Traveller's Almanack* came out in 1693, and was reprinted in 1694 and 1695; and this was followed by *The English Chapman's and Traveller's Almanack* in 1696, which was reprinted up to 1712. Similar publications appeared throughout the eighteenth century, many of them of a convenient size to

[1] Thomas Holcroft, *Memoirs*, London, 1926, p. 11. (First published 1816.)

slip into the pocket of the traveller. The information required by running stationers would concern routes and distances between towns and villages, together with details of fairs and markets held throughout the country. As the century went on, the task of the chapman was made very much easier by the spread of printing to the provincial towns. Chapbooks were produced in increasing numbers outside London, and as a result he was no longer dependent upon purchasing his wares in the capital, but could buy them from a local printer or dealer. It was, of course, not only chapmen who benefited from the spread of printing; it meant that children, too, had a much greater opportunity to purchase chapbooks direct from a local printer rather than await the arrival of the running stationer.

3

Printing in the provinces

In the eighteenth century printing spread to the provinces. The restrictions upon printers had finally lapsed in 1693, and during the ensuing hundred or so years, printers established themselves in increasing numbers outside the capital. There is no question of the pre-eminence of London as the chief centre of printing; but many local printers in both large and small towns up and down the country contributed very substantially to children's literature by producing cheap and often very attractive chapbooks for young readers.

After London, Newcastle upon Tyne was the earliest centre of chapbook printing. John White, son of the Royal Printer at York, had set up a printing press in the Close in 1711, and in the following year he moved to his 'House on the Side', where he remained in business for over half a century. 'There,' wrote the historian of Newcastle printing, 'developing a special line in broadsides and booklets, he announced that chapmen could be furnished with sermons, histories and ballads, etc.; and thither went peripatetic vendors of cheap literature for those treasuries of song, story and legend which formed the mental equipment of innumerable sons and daughters of toil throughout the northern counties.'

White, who was succeeded in business by Thomas Saint, also did a great deal of other printing. Saint was taken into partnership in 1761, and upon White's death in 1769 he carried on the printing concern until his own death in 1788. Besides printing an early Newcastle paper, he was noted as a chapbook printer and had a particularly fine stock of woodcuts quite apart from those which he commissioned from the young Thomas Bewick.

Thomas Angus, who was in business from about 1774, printed chapbooks which sometimes had hand-coloured woodcuts. He was succeeded by his wife and son, and his press was active until about 1825.

There were other chapbook printers in Newcastle, but the largest and best known was the firm founded by William Fordyce in about 1825. He enjoyed a considerable reputation as a chapbook printer, and shared this later with a partner, T. Fordyce; but whether this was a son or brother of the founder is not known. The founder died in 1863, and his partner in 1889, and although the business was continued for a short time, it did not long outlast the death of T. Fordyce.

Throughout almost the whole of the eighteenth century, and in much of the nineteenth, chapbooks were printed at Newcastle, and this proved to be not only the earliest but also the most productive provincial centre for the issue of chapbooks. Unfortunately few, if any, personal details of printers, publishers and booksellers have survived, and the considerable quantity of chapbooks printed in Newcastle which is still extant cannot even hint at the personalities of those who were active in their production.

After Newcastle, York. Although Thomas Gent printed chapbooks here, they were hardly suitable for children. He had been apprenticed to Edward Midwinter in London from about 1710 to 1713, and was a notable printer; but the man who specialized in children's chapbooks in this city was James Kendrew. He began printing in Colliergate in about 1803, and his output of books, many of which were particularly neatly printed, was very large. He employed his daughter and other female relatives to colour plates and valentines for him. Chapbooks with coloured illustrations belong almost entirely to the nineteenth century, and the colouring by hand of woodcuts was an operation which was often performed by children. There is a description of colouring these little prints in a forgotten Victorian book which enjoyed a good deal of popularity when it was first published[1]:

'Michael Bones, a poor artist once—poor in talent as in fortune—lives there. His art is some advantage, for by his six children's help, he gains a scanty livelihood for all as a print-colourer. There are little bones at work up there, not more than five years old, who colour prints, maps, or children's books from morning till night, and never play or chat about them. To them "Jack the Giant-Killer" is but so much work; and as each stands with his little colour-saucer before him, laying almost perpetually one streak of bright colour on the sheets of pictures which are before them, he wonders how happier children can take any pleasure in them, or think them pretty.'

The children of the Kendrew family were

[1] James Hain Friswell, *Houses with the fronts off*, London, 1854, p. 15.

perhaps more fortunate than those described above, for James Kendrew, who published an enormous number of chapbooks and broadsides, was a prosperous publisher; but the price at which these little coloured books were sold makes it likely that most of the colouring was done at starvation rates of pay, under conditions not dissimilar from those described by Friswell. The edition of *Cock Robin*, reproduced on pp. 145–160, provides a good example of Kendrew's work; both the printing and illustrations are well suited to young readers.

Kendrew continued in business until 1841, when his son John took it over, and after various other changes of ownership the firm was still in existence in 1874.

In other towns, too, printers of some note were at work. William Dicey, as we have seen, was in Northampton; and in towns like Birmingham, Sheffield, Worcester, Tewkesbury and Leicester there is evidence that chapbooks were being printed during the eighteenth century.

A more unlikely centre where there was a continuing tradition of chapbook printing was the little town of Banbury in Oxfordshire. Here, in about 1767, John Cheney set

THE

LIFE AND DEATH

OF

JENNY WREN.

A very small book,
  At a very small charge,
To learn them to read
  Before they grow large.

YORK:
Printed by J. Kendrew, Colliergate.

Front cover of a Kendrew chapbook printed in
the original on pale yellow paper.

up his printing press. As in the cases of so many printers, there are few records of his early life. There is a family tradition that he came from Great Rollright, a village twelve miles from Banbury, on the edge of the Cotswolds, where a record of his baptism on 4 March, 1732/3 is preserved in the parish registers. He started in business at the *Unicorn*, on the west side of the Market Place, and may well have been connected with brewing besides printing 'Bills' and 'Ballats'. Records for the early years of the firm exist, but they are extremely scanty. In 1771, Cheney was indicted for practising the art of printing without having served an apprenticeship; resourcefully, he apprenticed himself to John Madgeon, printer in the City of Oxford, but apparently only the letter of the law was obeyed and Cheney continued printing much as he had done before.

Most of this work was the usual jobbing that fell to a printer's lot in a small town— bills, notices, advertisements, sale catalogues, turnpike tickets, summonses and the like. In 1788 he left the *Unicorn* for premises in the 'upper End of Red Lion Street', where he described himself as a 'letterpress and copperplate printer, bookseller, stationer, and printseller'. His wares were diverse, and ranged from Bibles to bodkins, including playing-cards and garters.

Precisely when he commenced printing chapbooks is not known. As we have seen, 'ballats', or ballad sheets, were amongst the earliest items to come from his press, and two surviving broadsides were printed at the *Unicorn*, while most of the recorded chapbooks which are extant were printed after 1788, when Cheney moved. Those which give simply 'Banbury' as the place of origin probably appeared when Cheney had moved and expanded his business. It was at this period that he was advertising 'a good Assortment of Children's Books, Collections, Histories, Patters, Songs, Godly Books, etc., etc.'

One of the more interesting documents concerned with the Cheney business is a list of chapbooks and broadsides in possession of the firm, compiled at some date between 1808 and 1820. Not all were printed by Cheney, but the inventory gives a good idea of the stock of chapbooks held by a country book-seller in the early years of the nineteenth century. There are twenty-three chapbooks, amongst which many of the old favourites are represented; and there are also three titles listed as 'Children's Books': *House that Jack Built*, *The Apple Pye* and *Tom Thumb's plaything*. Even allowing for a considerable difference in demand between town and country, the total of twenty-three chapbooks held in stock by the Cheneys in the early nineteenth century marks something of a decline from the one hundred and fifty titles offered by Cluer Dicey and Richard Marshall in 1764, and throws some light upon the decline of the chapbook towards the close of the eighteenth century. Until about 1820 chapbooks were printed by Cheney's firm, which is still in existence in Banbury.

Another printer in this town made a speciality of children's books. This was J. G. Rusher, whose printing business lasted from 1803 to 1877. The Rusher family, in fact, was concerned in printing and bookselling in Banbury for over a century, William Rusher having been a bookseller and stationer in 1785, and one of the family, Philip, having patented a new kind of type which was used for an edition of Johnson's 'Rasselas' printed in 1804. Little is known of the individual members of the family, whose numerous tiny chapbooks for children were amongst the most important of their productions. The

42

Rusher edition of *Children in the Wood*, reproduced on pp. 129–144, typifies the high standard of their publications.

Two firms in Nottingham made a feature of printing and selling chapbooks. One was founded by George Burbage in 1772, and from his 'Patter, Song and History Warehouse' he issued a number of chapbooks. A few of those which are dated appeared in 1779, 1792, 1794 and 1796, but most of his output was undated. The other Nottingham printer of this period was Charles Sutton, who commenced in business in about 1794, the firm remaining in existence for over seventy-five years. Both Burbage and Sutton printed local newspapers, and because of their activities Nottingham at the end of the eighteenth century became an important centre for the printing of chapbooks, and remained so for the next twenty years or so.

In Manchester and Coventry also there were well-known chapbook printers. George Swindells, who came from Disley, Cheshire, was born in 1760, and in the last quarter of the eighteenth century he ran a printing office in Hanging Bridge from which he issued chapbooks and broadsides. The penny histories were usually of sixteen pages, printed upon coarse paper, with woodcut illustrations. When he died in 1796 the business was continued by A. Swindells and his son John, who died in 1853, although he had ceased printing chapbooks some years before his death. 'I have a vivid remembrance,' wrote 'W.H.' in *The Manchester Guardian,* 'of their well-known windows fronting the pathway leading to and opposite the present Cathedral.' Nearly all the favourite chapbook titles were printed and sold by Swindells, and in addition, he printed several of purely local interest.

John Turner, the Coventry chapbook printer, was born in 1773, and died aged ninety in 1863. From his premises, at one time located in the High Street, there came a number of chapbooks, none of which is dated, although there is some reason to believe that these and other ephemeral popular literature were issued between 1790 and 1840. Turner supplied 'shopkeepers and travellers with all sorts of histories, new and old ballads, Godly and other patters, carols, Cock Robin, Tom Thumb, London cries and various other playbooks for children on reasonable terms'; and he was, according to his obituary notice in *The Coventry Herald and*

Observer, '. . . for many years . . . a respectable printer and bookseller . . . .'

There can have been few towns of any size or importance in early nineteenth-century England where there was not at least one printer amongst whose productions would be two or three small books for children.

Eighteenth-century chapbooks, however, must be considered in a wider context than the lack of scholarly attention they have so far received seems to suggest. Neglect of this important branch of cultural history has tended to obscure and even invalidate any assessment of the ability to read amongst the poor in eighteenth-century England. The considerable extent of the chapbook trade in London, and its gradual though perceptible development in provincial towns throughout the Augustan period, are important facts of social history. A detailed study of chapbooks and elementary education[1] certainly calls in question the loosely held assumption that the poor were almost entirely unlettered[2] at this time, and shows that the mass reading public which was a feature of Victorian England had substantial roots in the preceding century.

[1] Such a study has been completed by the present writer in a research project carried out under the auspices of the University of Leicester.

[2] See, for example, R. D. Altick, *The English Common Reader*, University of Chicago Press, 1957, p. 29.

4

Chapbooks in America

In America chapbooks never achieved the enormous popularity that they enjoyed in Great Britain; neither did they play such an important part in the culture of that country. None the less, from about 1725 to 1825 large numbers of chapbooks and broadsides were circulated, usually by pedlars who, as in this country, supplied the everyday necessities to isolated farms and settlements. After the Revolution both lost ground to the increasing volume of daily and weekly newspapers which began to appear in all the American States.

The earliest chapbooks which were read in America were imported from England, and it was not until about 1755 to 1760 that Messrs. Fowle and Draper, printers in Boston, probably began printing chapbooks. They kept numerous titles in stock in order to supply the many chapmen, but it is by no means certain how many of these were printed in America, and how many were imported.

In Philadelphia, Andrew Steuart, who dealt

in chapbooks and printed some besides importing them, was in business from about 1763 to 1765; and it was not only in the larger cities of Boston, Philadelphia and New York that printers of chapbooks were to be found, for presses were often set up in much smaller towns. In New London, for example, J. Green was at work from about 1754 to 1757, and he was responsible for printing several chapbooks.

These early chapbooks were very similar to their English counterparts, and it seems certain that American children found them as enthralling as young English readers did— and, remembering the strictly Protestant, and even Puritan, background of Colonial days, for very much the same reasons.

American chapbooks fell into two broad categories: first there were the traditional titles, printed in America from English versions; then there were those of specifically American interest, the most characteristic of these being the 'Indian Captivity' titles[1], of which many hundreds appeared in typical chapbook style. These were narratives of adventure and hardship told by captives who

[1] One of the earliest of these is *Mary Rowlandson's Captivity*, Cambridge, Mass., 1682.

had escaped from the Indians—although by no means all the exploits in them were authentic. A few 'captivities' found their way to England and Scotland, where they were published in London, Glasgow, Stirling and other cities. Typical titles were: *A Narrative of the Sufferings and Surprizing Deliverance of William and Elizabeth Fleming, Who were taken captive by Capt. Jacob, Commander of the Indians, etc.*, 1756; or *The Affecting history of dreadful distresses of Frederick Manheim's family, to which are added an encounter between a white man and two savages . . .*, n.d. (1792-93).

Many of these titles were widely read, and went through several editions. They were the forerunners of the 'Western' adventure story which has continued to be popular not only in book form but also in the media of comic strip, film and television. The appeal to children of such tales was as real in the eighteenth century as it is today, and these books would have found some of their most avid readers amongst the young.

One of the most popular captivity tales was called *A very surprising narrative of a young woman, discovered in a rocky-cave, after having been taken by the savage Indians of the wilderness in the year* 1777, *and seeing no human being for the*

49

space of nine years. In a letter from a gentleman to his friend. This was written by 'Abraham Panther', and several editions of it appeared between about 1786 and 1816.

In the story, two travellers on a journey through the Western wilderness discovered, to their tremendous astonishment, 'a most beautiful young lady sitting near the mouth of a cave'. Since she was singing, she did not see the approach of the visitors until the barking of a dog warned her of their proximity. Upon seeing them she screamed and fainted dead away. She soon recovered and exclaimed, 'Heavens! Where am I? And who, and from whence are you?' There was some conversation, and when she was convinced that no harm would come to her, she told her story. Her father was a wealthy man, and she had been born near Albany in 1760. She fell in love with one of her father's clerks, 'a young man of easy politeness, good sense and agreeable manners'. At first her father, being too busy in the pursuit of riches, did not notice the attachment of the two young people; but when he did, he dismissed the clerk and ordered his daughter to stay at home. Through the good offices of a servant they managed to elope, but were both captured by Indians who burned the young man at the stake. The girl escaped from her captors, having cut off the head of her guard and hacked his body into quarters. She then stayed for nine years in the cave to which she had been brought, and lived upon the Indian corn she cultivated, alone except for the company of a dog. The travellers took the young lady home, where there was a touching reunion with her father, who fainted at the sight of her. Upon recovering, he listened to his daughter's tale; but he had only a few more minutes to live, and having heard her story he died, leaving a considerable fortune to the young lady.

The best-known author of such tales was Josiah Priest, born at Unadilla, New York, in 1788. He managed to combine with authorship the trades of coach-trimmer and harness-maker, and his work as an early historian of the American frontier, as well as a writer of these Indian captivities, was extremely popular. Priest died in 1851, and of thousands of copies of his pamphlets, only a few have survived.

Two book-pedlars, or chapmen, deserve mention. The first is Chapman Whitcomb, who was born in Massachusetts in 1765. At the age of twenty he graduated from Dartmouth College with an interest in literary pursuits. He became, however, a peripatetic teacher of English, and to supplement his income he published chapbooks, some of which were probably printed for him by C. Prentiss and S. Wilder with various associates who ran a jobbing press at Leominster, Mass., from 1796 to 1813. The chapbooks which he sold on his travels were varied, consisting of religious and moral tales, biography, adventure, geography and other topics, and including 'captivities'; and occasionally his own works appeared in chapbook form. In addition to publishing and selling, Whitcomb lent money on property and worked for some time as a carpenter. Known as an eccentric character, he died in 1833.

Better known than Whitcomb was Mason Locke Weems, inventor of the George Washington cherry-tree tale, who between 1795 and his death in 1825, travelled in rural and urban areas between New York and Georgia distributing the pamphlets he had written. These, because of their title-pages and contents, should in fact be classed as chapbooks. Weems—known as Parson

Weems—was a student of medicine besides being ordained, and he was one of the most active clergymen in Maryland, combining preaching and bookselling with an energy which was reminiscent of John Wesley's.

At the beginning of the nineteenth century, amongst several publishers and booksellers issuing chapbooks for children[1], three New York firms were the most important figures in this trade. These were Samuel Wood, Mahlon Day and Solomon King.

Samuel Wood was born on Long Island in 1760. He was a schoolmaster until the age of forty, when he found that he could not support a family on a teacher's pay, and went into the second-hand book business. His experiences led him to believe that many children's books were unsuitable for young readers, and so he decided to print children's books which he himself had written or compiled. The first of these, *The Young Child's ABC, or, First Book*, was published in 1806, and by 1813 he had nearly '50 kinds of little books of his own printing'.

[1] The distinction between a chapbook and a small paper-covered child's book is extremely fine, and such were the physical characteristics and contents of tiny, ephemeral books designed for children that it seems reasonable to regard them as chapbooks.

THE

NEW-YORK CRIES,

IN RHYME.

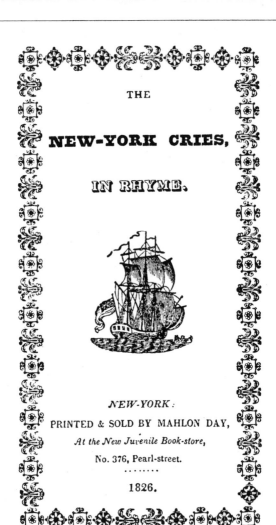

NEW-YORK:

PRINTED & SOLD BY MAHLON DAY,

At the New Juvenile Book-store,

No. 376, Pearl-street.

. . . .

1826.

The publishing business was so successful that in 1810 and again in 1817 he had to move into larger premises. Various sons were taken into partnership, and the founder retired in 1836 and died eight years later. The children's books published by Samuel Wood were distinctly moral in tone, and were generally illustrated, some of them selling for as little as three cents a copy. In general they lacked the attractive qualities of fairy tales and old romances, and bore a somewhat depressing similarity to the books which were popular in England at this time, written by the imitators of Hannah More and 'the cursed Barbauld Crew, those Blights and Blasts of all that is Human in man and child', as Lamb characterized them.

The books published by Mahlon Day were very similar to Wood's. In all of them there was a tendency to piety and virtue; they were designed first to be instructive, and then entertaining. Usually they were illustrated, and sometimes the illustrations were in colour. Day, born in New Jersey in 1790, was in business from about 1816 to about 1845. He was no innovator with children's books, and all his publications of this kind show the pervasive influence of the 'moral tale'; some, indeed, were directly patterned upon the English publications which had, by the beginning of the nineteenth century, to some extent superseded the penny histories, and in which frivolity was deplored, and the purpose of books for children, far from delighting the reader, was to point out moral obligations and inspire religious feeling. The similarity between such literature and the traditional chapbooks is to be found in appearance only, and certainly not in their contents.

One of the more interesting features of Mahlon Day's books was the way in which he used to include a rhymed advertisement for his publications in some of them. In *The Penny Primer* we find:

> 'I had three cents to spend
> I ran to Day's with glee
> To get a picture book;
> And here I've got it—see!'

And in *Simple Stories* there is the following:

> 'Of all the stores in New York city
> Day's is the one for Toys,
> Many there are in prose or ditty
> For either Girls or Boys.'

Day referred to his little books as 'toys', and this was probably an abbreviation of the term 'toy-book' which was sometimes used in England. Such enterprise in the promotion of his books, however, does not relieve the general dullness which pervades both his publications and those of Wood. It is the illustrations alone which give them charm.

Solomon King, bookseller and publisher of children's books from about 1821 to 1832, issued many books for amusement rather than instruction. Not many of his publications have survived, and they are known simply because they were advertised in the few remaining books of his which are to be found in the New York Public Library and elsewhere. From these, Harry B. Weiss has been able to reconstruct an admirable account of King's publishing activities.

In 1828 King was advertising one hundred and sixty titles. Of these, over half were fairy tales, fiction, nursery stories, and only one-seventh could be described as religious or moral. Several chapbooks, including *Valentine and Orson*, *The Life of Dr. Faustus*, *Robin Hood* and *The Life of Bamfyld Moore Carew*, were listed, and this was one of the last occasions on which the traditional chapbooks were offered for sale in America. From the example included in this volume it can be seen how the chapbook style was adapting itself to the demands of the new century. It is written almost in the manner of an educational 'reader' and its plain but attractive approach to a world of facts bears a notable relationship to the multifarious writings of 'Peter Parley' which became such a prominent feature of the American and European scene from 1827 onwards.

There were, of course, other publishers of chapbooks after the Revolution, notably in New York, Philadelphia and Boston; but by the time printing was well established in America, the decline of the traditional chapbook at the close of the eighteenth century had begun.

James Catnach and the chapbook revival

Towards the end of the eighteenth century, as we have seen, chapbooks began to go out of fashion amongst adult readers. The reasons for this were complex, and intimately related to a change in man's outlook occasioned by the more tangible evidences of the industrial revolution which was impinging upon their lives at this period. The far-reaching changes in the structure of society which began to obtrude into men's consciousness during the last two decades of the eighteenth century changed, profoundly and beyond all recognition, the values and attitudes which had been part of their traditional way of life in a pre-industrial society.

From this it followed that a labourer in one of the rapidly growing towns in the industrial North of England was no longer content with the old romances, with *Fortunatus* or *The Seven Champions of Christendom*. Smarting under the injustices of an often brutal system,

VALENTINE & ORSON

NEW JUVENILE LIBRARY.

THE

ADVENTURES

OF

VALENTINE AND ORSON.

EMBELLISHED WITH

Four Elegant Copperplates.

A NEW AND CORRECT EDITION.

LONDON:

PRINTED FOR THE BOOKSELLERS,

1816.

and unable to understand the break-up of an old way of life and the fragmentation of his own pattern of existence, he was more ready to turn to a paper-covered copy of Thomas Paine's *Rights of Man*, or to other political pamphlets. This may suggest a sense of bewilderment rather than a revolutionary impulse or an understanding of what was happening in society. It was to lead to the dawning of a new consciousness, a new awareness of the working man's place in the scheme of things, and thus to a demand for a fresh kind of literature which would provide not romantic escape but knowledge by means of which he could come to terms with and ultimately master his new environment. In the long run, however, it was probably popular fiction in a somewhat different form —fiction descending from 'horrid' Gothic novels, through the shorter tales of Isaac Crookenden and others to Edward Lloyd's penny dreadfuls and 'Bow Bells' novelettes— which had wider influence in reshaping the attitudes and values of a rapidly growing reading public than the more didactic literature offered by Lord Brougham's Society for the Diffusion of Useful Knowledge, or the radical pamphlets of William Hone. While it

Front cover of a mid-nineteenth century provincial
chapbook crudely printed in three colours.

is impossible not to admire the immense courage of Richard Carlile, who combined radical and free-thought publishing, it is doubtful whether his publications reached a fraction of those who read sensational fiction. It was left to G. W. M. Reynolds, later in the nineteenth century, to unite a deeply felt moral indignation at social injustice and repression with a talent for writing sensational stories which were widely enjoyed in his own day.

The more immediate, though by no means the least important, result of these changes in society was that the eighteenth-century chapbook declined in popularity, although it did not disappear altogether; while so far as children were concerned these years saw the beginning of a return to the stark didacticism which had been almost the only distinguishing feature of seventeenth-century authors like James Janeway. Round about 1780 authors began to be commissioned to write for young readers, and books by Mrs. Trimmer, Mrs. Barbauld, Dorothy and Mary Jane Kilner and Lady Eleanor Fenn were published. Soon afterwards, in 1818, Mrs. Sherwood published *The History of the Fairchild Family*; and her hell-fire and brimstone morality often became archness and insipidity in the hands of her numerous successors, who were lacking not in piety but in the obsessive and articulate moral fervour which had driven the creator of the Fairchilds. One of the few exceptions to this depressing development was the work of the Taylors of Ongar which, though no less moral and instructive in tone, was nevertheless relieved by considerable charm and insight into the minds of the young readers for whom it was intended. Maria Edgeworth's tales, too, while retaining the moral flavour of the day, were notable for their author's skill in narrative and pleasing characterization.

As we have seen, several printers in provincial towns were printing chapbooks for children during the seventeen-eighties and seventeen-nineties, and continued to do so during the first decades of the nineteenth century; but the heyday of the chapbook was over. It was no longer the most important element in popular literature; and it was now entirely intended for child readers.

Religious tracts were produced in ever-increasing numbers—the Religious Tract Society, which had been founded in 1799, published many titles. Despite a superficial resemblance to chapbooks, the contents could not have been more unlike those of the penny histories, of whose traditional popularity the tract producers clearly wished to take advantage. Perhaps the most ambitious of the publications at this time which contrived to look like rather superior, even pretentious descendants of the cheaper and humbler chapbook were the sixpenny series of 'Juvenile Books . . . with Neat Embellishments'. These were issued, undated but probably around 1860, by Oliver and Boyd, with clear print and well executed woodcut illustrations. There were more than forty-five titles in the series, ranging from *Jack the Giant-Killer* to *The Child's Manual of Devotion*.

One printer who did more than anyone to realize the potentialities of the chapbook, despite the fashion for morality, to amuse and delight young readers was James Catnach. His achievement in providing cheap books for children, and attractive textbooks by means of which they could learn the ABC and reading through the medium of nursery rhymes, has generally been unregarded. Catnach is chiefly recalled as the printer of Seven Dials who specialized in printing street ballads and execution sheets. *Confession and*

Execution of William Corder, the Murderer of Maria Marten was one of his more successful titles, and at a time when newspapers were highly priced, Catnach provided something of a service, if only with the more sensational items of news. The resourcefulness shown by him in the production and circulation of 'gallows literature' and street songs was equalled by his energy in providing cheap and attractive juvenile literature which, like the chapbooks of a century earlier, was designed to delight rather than instruct with the heavy-handed piety which had lain like a dead weight upon so many early children's books.

James Catnach had been born in Alnwick, Northumberland, in 1792. His father was a printer, who was associated at one time with William Davison and had employed Bewick the engraver. The elder Catnach had various ups and downs in his business affairs, and he died in St. George's Hospital, Hyde Park Corner, where he had been ill for fourteen weeks. To his son James he left little more than the press he had used at Alnwick, and later in Newcastle and London, together with a small supply of type and woodcuts. With this equipment James Catnach took premises

67

at No. 2 Monmouth Court, Seven Dials, in 1813[1], and set up as a jobbing printer, dealing in penny histories, street papers of all kinds, and song sheets. The output of the 'Catnach Press' was enormous, and there is a legend that his kitchen behind the printing office was 'papered' with the bad pennies paid to him by trade customers. All the hawkers and less reputable dealers who did business with him —so the story goes—paid him in coppers which he used to take to the Bank of England, packed in large bags, in a hackney coach, because most of his neighbours, knowing from whom he had received them, dreaded to take the coins in case they were infected. His somewhat eccentric manner of dress occasioned some comment, but even by those who stigmatized him as 'dirty and ignorant' his enterprise was admitted.

The children's books issued by Catnach ranged in price from one farthing for a tiny one to a halfpenny for a slightly larger book, while a large quarto cost one penny. The titles were many, and varied considerably: *Jack Spratt*, *Cock Robin*, *Mother Goose*, *Simple Simon*, *Dick Turpin*, *Moll Flanders*, *Tom*

---

[1] In 1883, the whole area was pulled down to make way for a new road.

Hickathrift, Jack Sheppard, The Tragical Death of an Apple Pie, Cinderella, and a host of others. His advertisement which spoke of 'A Variety of Children's Books' was, if anything, an understatement.

Catnach's juvenile publications were attractive in both contents and appearance. Not only were they free of the moralizing tendency we have already deplored, but they were as a rule well illustrated, and could hardly fail to have had a tremendous appeal for young readers of all classes. He was not an educated man, and had received an intermittent and unsatisfactory education in Alnwick, but like William Dicey almost exactly a century earlier, Catnach possessed an instinctive flair for assessing public demand and then satisfying it with a variety of cheap publications which provided him with a speedy and increasingly large financial return.

In 1838 Catnach retired from business and went to live at South Mimms, near Barnet. Three years later he died. Upon his retirement his sister, Mrs. Ryle, took over the management, and she was assisted by a James Paul who had risen from being Catnach's apprentice to the position of manager. Ultimately the Catnach Press was purchased

69

by Mr. W. S. Fortey, who ran it until about 1883. A trade announcement issued by him gives some idea of the scope of this long-established firm:

'*The Catnach Press* (Established 1813)

'William S. Fortey (late A. Ryle, successor to the late J. Catnach), Printer, Publisher and Wholesale Stationer, 2 and 3 Monmouth Court, Seven Dials, London, W.C.

'The cheapest and greatest variety in the trade of large coloured penny books; half-penny coloured books; farthing books; penny and half-penny panoramas; school books; poetry cards; lotteries; ballads (4,000 sorts) and hymns; scripture sheets; Christmas pieces; Twelfth-night characters; books and sheet almanacks; envelopes; note paper, etc.'

Because of Catnach, chapbooks enjoyed a remarkable revival. As a pioneer in the production of cheap books for children, he was unrivalled in the nineteenth century, and the fact that he had imitators simply meant that there was a greater variety of cheaply priced books available for young readers. His was a unique achievement, and his service to children was immeasurable—the paradox is that he was a bachelor, and had no family of his own. None of his publications was original, but he kept alive the tradition of fairy tales and nursery rhymes when too many authors felt that they had a solemn duty to re-write or suppress them in the interests of a more overtly moral and improving literature.

Toads and Diamonds, reproduced in this volume, is a good example of Catnach's staunch support of traditional tales. The lettering and the portico of its cover may betray its nineteenth-century origin, but the story is yet another version of a tale common throughout Europe since the Middle Ages. One of its earliest appearances in print for children (and certainly its most famous) was in Perrault's collection where it has the title *Les Fées.* This was translated as *The Fairy* in the first English edition of *Histories or Tales of Times Past,* which was published in 1729.

Chapbooks enjoyed another, minor revival in the hands of George Mogridge[1], an evangelical writer who wrote a remarkably large number of books for children. Most of these were published by the Religious Tract Society, although his work appeared under

[1] He was born near Birmingham in 1787 and died at Hastings in 1854.

no less than seven other imprints. Harvey
Darton recalls George Mogridge as 'a Proteus
of the Early Victorian Juvenile Library', and
mentions that he wrote under the pseudo-
nyms of 'Peter Parley', 'Ephraim Holding'
and 'Old Humphrey'. It was under this last
name that he was probably best known to his
young readers, although many of his books
appeared anonymously. 'He had,' wrote
Harvey Darton, 'been brought up on chapbook literature—*Friar Bacon*, *The Seven Champions* and *Tom Thumb*.'

Mogridge himself refers to these romances
in a poem he wrote later in life:

'And did the magic of romantic lays
Seduce the leisure of my earlier days?
And has the midnight taper wasted been
In pondering legend hoar, and fairy scene?
Have idle fictions o'er my fancy stole
And superstition's tale beguiled my soul?
They have; and spell'd by their mysterious
    power
Has roll'd away full many a rosy hour.
Farewell, ye tales of terror, that control
In mystic bonds the passions of the soul.
Ye fabled haunts, where fays and genii dwell,
And all ye legendary themes, farewell.

Your fleeting joys I freely now resign;
For ever let the Book of Truth be mine. '

His own views on what children's books
ought to be were admirably succinct:

'. . . Young people require a proper mixture of
grave and gay to edify them.'

His own books and chapbooks, however,
were hardly written in this spirit. There was
gravity and edification in them, but of gaiety
one finds little trace. In many of them he was
clearly reacting against 'idle fictions' and
'fleeting joys', and on at least one occasion
he went out of his way to criticize *Tom
Thumb* as being likely to corrupt children.

There would be little to distinguish George
Mogridge from other early nineteenth-century writers for children, had it not been for
the fact that he wrote chapbooks for them,
doubtless remembering the more robust ones
that he had read as a child. They were, of
course, little more than religious tracts, but
they so resembled chapbooks in appearance,
and there were so many of them, that they
should be mentioned. Those published by

the Religious Tract Society included fifty-three little 32mo books, with covers and pictures, costing one farthing each; fifteen half-penny titles, and eight at one penny each. In addition to this total, there were fourteen unpriced tracts, two books price three-half-pence, a twopenny one and ten fourpenny titles. He also wrote, for the firm of Houlston, at least one series of 'Juvenile Tracts, for the amusement and improvement of Young Persons', with woodcut illustrations typical of the early nineteenth-century chapbook tradition.

It would be idle to pretend that George Mogridge's writing possesses any enduring quality, or that it has been unjustly overlooked and allowed to sink into an undeserved oblivion. Neither is it fair nor relevant to dismiss him, in the words of a contemporary, as a 'sanctimonious humbug'. The children's books of George Mogridge are typical of the lower reaches of nineteenth-century evangelicism, and are certainly preferable to the morbid excesses of Mrs. Sherwood. His interest lies in the fact that he consciously attempted to adapt the traditional chapbook as a medium for his own religious and moral teaching. He was not the only

74

person to do this, but he was certainly the most prolific writer of such little books, and for this reason, if for no other, he deserves a niche in the history of chapbooks.

The facsimile which has been included here from the Houlston series is not entirely typical of 'Old Humphrey's' chapbook style. His moralizings often flow from a more dramatic narrative than *The Rod,* but this particular example has a more varied set of woodcuts than usual, while the text provides a view of child-guidance worth comparing with that of Mr. Fairchild (whose creator likewise published many of her tracts through Houlston).

As we have seen, James Catnach was very largely responsible for the revival of the chapbook. By the time that W. S. Fortey—last owner of the Catnach Press—went out of business in the eighteen-eighties, the day of the chapbook was done; its place had been taken by the penny dreadful—Varney the Vampire had superseded Fortunatus.

For almost two centuries children had delighted in chapbooks. Intended in the first instance for adults, the content and convenient size of these books had made an immediate appeal to young readers. Today, many

*The pinnace brings **bad news**.*

The enduring tradition: a 'chapbook' purchased new in 1953—*Grenville of the Revenge* by John Richmond.

chapbook heroes of romance and fairy tale continue to enjoy an undiminished popularity; if Guy of Warwick is forgotten, Robin Hood has reached a wider public than ever, while Simple Simon and Jack the Giant-Killer are household names. Despite competition from all kinds of fiction and the comic strip, chapbook literature endures as a robust tradition which shows no sign of coming to an end; and a diligent search of newsagents' shops **may** still reveal small paper-bound editions of fairy tales and nursery rhymes priced at a copper or two, which to the initiated eye bear a faint resemblance to the penny histories from which they are descended.

Facsimile reproductions

THE
HISTORY
OF
GUY, Earl of Warwick.

Printed and Sold in Aldermary Church
Yard, London

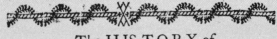

The HISTORY of

GUY, Earl of Warwick.

CHAP. I.

Guy's Praise. He falls in Love with
Fair Phillis.

IN the blessed time when Athelstone
wore the crown of the English nation,e
Sir Guy, Warwick's mirror, and all the
world's wonder, was the chief hero of the
age ; whose process so surpassed all his
predecessors, that the trump of fame so
loudly sounded Warwick's praise, that
Jews, Turks, and Infidels became acquainted with his name.

But as Mars the God of Battle was inspired with the beauty of Venus, so our Guy, by no means conquered, was conquered by love; for Phillis the fair, whose beauty and virtue were inestimable, shining with such heavenly lustre, that Guy's poor heart was ravished in adoration of this heavenly Phillis, whose beauty was so ecellent, that Helen the pride of all Greece, might seem as a Black-a-Moor to her.

Guy resolving not to stand doating at a distance, went to Warwick Castle, where Phillis dwelt, being daughter and heiress to the Earl of Warwick; the Earl her father hearing of Guy's coming, entertained him with great joy; after some time the Earl invited Guy to go a hunting with him; but he finding himself unable to partake of the diversion feigned himself sick. The Earl trouble for his friend Guy, sent his own Physician to him. The Doctor told Guy his disease was dangerous, and without letting blood there was no remedy. Guy replied, I know my body is distempered; but you want skill to cure the inward inflammation of my heart; Galen's herbal cannot quote the flower I like for my remedy : I know my own difease, Doctor, and am obliged to you.

The Doctor departed, and left Guy to caft his eyes on the heavenly face of his Phillis, as fhe was walking in a garden full of rofes and other flowers.

CHAP. II.

Guy courts fair Phillis, fhe at firft denies, but after grants his Suit on Conditions, which he accepts.

GUY immediately advanced to fair Phillis, who was repofing herfelf in an arbour, and faluted her with bended knees, All hail, fair Phillis, flower of beauty, and jewel of virtue, I know great princes feek to win thy love, whofe exquifite perfections might grace the mightieft monarch in the world ; yet may they come fhort of Guy's real affection ; in whom love is pictured with naked truth and honesty, disdain me not for being a steward's son, one of thy father's servants.

Phillis interrupted him, saying, Cease, bold youth, leave off this passionate address:—You are but young and meanly born, and unfit for my degree: I would not my father should know this:

Guy, thus discomfited, lived like one distracted, wringing his hands, resolving to travel through the world to gain the love of Phillis, or death to end his misery. Long may dame Fortune frown, but when her course is run she sends a smile to cure the hearts that have been wounded by her frowns; so Cupid sent a powerful dart, representing to her a worthy Knight of chivalry, saying, This Knight shall become so famous in the world, that his

actions shall crown everlasting posterity.
When Phillis found herself wounded, she
cried, O pity me gentle Cupid, follicit for
me to thy mother, and I will offer myself
up at thy shrine.

Guy little dreaming of this so sudden
thaw, and wanting the balm of love to
apply to his sores, resolves to make a second encounter. So coming again to his
Phillis, said, Fair Lady, I have been ar-
raigned long ago, and now am come to
receive my just sentence from the Tribu-
nal of Love : It is life or death fair Phillis, I look for , let me not languish in
despair, give Judgment, O ye fair, give
Judgment, that I may know my doom :
a word from thy sacred lips can cure my
bleeding heart, or a frown can doom me
to the pit of misery. Gentle Guy, said
she, I am not at my own disposal, you
know my fathers name is great in the
nation, and I dare not match without his
consent.

Sweet Lady, said Guy, I make no doubt
but quickly to obtain his love and favour.
let me have thy love first, fair Phillis,
and there is no fear of thy father's wrath
preventing us. It is an old saying, Get

the good-will of the daughter, and that of the parent will soon follow.

Sir Guy, quoth Phillis, make thy bold atchievements and noble actions shine abroad, glorious as the sun, that all opposers may tremble at thy high applauded name and then thy suit cannot be denied.

Fair Phillis, said Guy, I ask no more. — Never did the hound mind more his game, than I do this my new enterprize. Phillis, take thy farewell, end accept of this kiss as the signet of my heart.

CHAP

C H A P. III.

Guy wins the Emperor's Daughter from several Princes. He is set upon by sixteen Assassins, whom he overcomes.

THUS noble Guy, at last disengaged from Love's cruelty, he now arms himself like a Knight of Chivalry, and crossing the raging ocean, he quickly arrived at the court of Thrace, where he heard that the Emperor of Almain's fair daughter Blanch, was to be made a prize for him that won her in the field; upon which account the worthies of the world assembled to try their fortunes.——The golden trumpets sounded with great joy and triumph, and the stately pampered steeds prance over the ground, and each He there thought himself a Cæsar, that none could equal; Kings and Princes being there, to behold who should be the conqueror, every one thinking that fair Blanch should be his.

After desperate charging with horse and man, much blood was shed, and Princes no more valued than vulgar perfons; but our noble Guy appearing, laid about him like a lion, among the princes; here lay one headlefs, another without a leg or an arm, and there a horfe.——Guy ft.ll like Hercules, charged defperately and killed a German Prince and his horfe under him. Duke Otto vowing revenge upon our Englifh champion, gave Guy a frefh

affault, but his courage was foon cooled Then Duke Poyner would engage our favourite Knight; but with as little fuc- cefs as the reft, fo that no man could en- counter Guy any more; by which valor he won the Lady in the field as a prize, being the approved conqueror.

The Emperor being himfelf a fpecta- tor, he fent a meffenger for our Englifh knight.—Guy immediately came into the Emperor's presence, and made his obeysance, when the Emperor as a token of his affection, gave him his hand to kiss, and

withal resigned him his daughter, the falcon and the hound.—Guy thanked his Majesty for his gracious favour, but for fair Phillis's sake, left fair Blanch to her father's tuition, and departed from that graceful court only with the other tokens of victory.

Now Guy beginning to meditate upon his long absence from his fair Phillis, and doubting of her prosperity, or that she might too much forget him, because the proverb says, Out of Sight, out of Mind! prepared for England, and at last arrived at the long-wished for haven of his love;

and' with this sort of salutation greeted
his beloved mistress: Fair foe, said he,
I am now come to challenge your promise, the which was, upon my making
my name famous by martial deeds, I
should be the master of my beloved mistress. — Behold fair Phillis, part of the
prize I have won in the field before Kings
and princes.

Worthy Knight, quoth Phillis, I have
heard of thy winning the Lady Blanch
from Royal Dukes and Princes, and I am
glad to find that Guy is so victorious.
But indeed Guy thou must seek more
adventures.

Guy, discomfited at this answer, taking leave of his fair Phillis, clad himself
again in Belona's livery, and travelled towards Sedgwin, Duke of Nouvain, against
whom the Emperor of Almain had then
laid siege. But as Guy was going his intended journey, Duke Otto, whom Guy
had disgraced in battle, hired sixteen base
traytors to slay him. Guy being set upon by these rogues, drew his sword, and
fought till he had slain them all ; and
leaving their carcasses to the fowls of the
air, he pursued his Journey to Louvain,

which he found close besieged, and little
resistance could the Duke make against
the Emperor's power.—Guy caused the
Levinians to sally forth, and made a most
bloody slaughter amongst the Almains;
but the Emperor gathering more forces
renewed the siege, thinking to starve
them out; but Guy in another sally defeated the Almains, slaying in these two
battles about thirteen thousand men,

After this Guy made a perfect league
between the Emperor and the Duke,
gaining more praise thereby than by his
former victories.

C H A P.

C H A P. IV.

Guy having performed great Wonders
Abroad, returns to England, and is
married to Phillis.

AFter a tedious journey Guy fat down
by a fpring to refrefh himfelf, and
he foon heard a hedious noife, and pre-
fently efpied a Lion and a Dragon fight-
ing, biting, and tearing each other ; but
Guy perceiving the Lion ready to faint,
encountered the Dragon, and foon brought
the ugly Cerberes roaring and yelling to
the ground. — The Lion in gratitude to
Guy, run by his horfe's fide like a true-
born fpaniel, till lack of food made him
retire to his wonted abode.

Soon after Guy met with the Earl of Terry, whose father was confined in his castle by Duke Otto; but he and that Lord posted thither, and freed the castle immediately; and Guy in an open field slew Duke Otto hand to hand; but his dying words of repentance moved Guy to remorse and pity.

But as Guy returned through a desart, he met a furious boar that had slain many Christians. Guy manfully drew his sword and the boar gaping, intending with his

dreadful tusks to devour our noble champion; but Guy run it down his throat, and slew the greatest boar, that ever man beheld.

At Guy's arrival in England, he immediately repaired to King Athelstone at

York, where the King told Guy of a mighty Dragon in Northumberland, that destroyed men, women, and children. — Guy desired a guide, and went immediately to the dragon's cave, when out came the monster, with eyes like flaming fire; Guy charged him courageously; but the monster bit the lance in two like a reed; then Guy drew his sword, and cut such gashes in the dragons sides that the blood and life poured out of his venemous carcase. Then Guy cut off the head of the monster, and presented it to the King, who in the memory of Guy's service caused the picture of the Dragon, being thirty feet in length to be worked in a cloth of arras, and hung up in Warwick Castle for an everlasting monument.

Phillis hearing of Guy's return and success, came as far as Lincoln to meet him, where they were married with much joy and great triumph; King Athelstone, his Queen, the chief Nobles and Barons of the land being present.

No sooner were their nuptials celebrated, but Phillis's father died leaving all his estate to Sir Guy; and the King made him Earl of Warwick.

C H A P. V,
Guy leaves his Wife, and goes a Pilgrimage to the Holy Land.

IN the very height of Guy's glory, being exalted to his fathers dignities, Conscience biddeth him repent of all his former sins, and his youthful time, spent in the behalf of women; so Guy resolved to travel to the Holy Land like a Pilgrim. Phillis perceiving this sudden alteration, enquires of her Lord what was the cause of this passion?—Ah! Phillis, said he, I have spent much time in honouring thee, and to win thy favour, but never spared one minute for my soul's health in honouring the Lord.

Phillis, though very much grieved, understanding his determination, opposed not his will. So with exchanging their rings, and melting kisses, he departed, like a stranger from his own habitation, taking neither money nor scrip with him, and but a small quantity of herbs and roots, such only as the wild fields could

afford, where his chief diet ; vowing never to fight more but in a juſt cauſe.

Guy, after travelling many tedious
miles, met an aged perſon oppreſſed with
grief, for the loſs of fifteen ſons, whom
Armarant, a mighty Giant had taken
from him, and held in ſtrong captivity.

Guy borrowed the old man's ſword, and
went directly up to the caſtle gate, where
the Giant dwelt, who coming to the door,
aſked grimly, How he durſt ſo boldly
knock at the gates ? vowing he would
beat his brains out. But Guy laughing
at him, ſaid, Sirrah, thou art quarrel-
ſome ; — but I have a ſword has often
hewn ſuch lubbards as you aſunder : —
At the ſame time laying his blade about
the Giant's ſhoulders, that he bled abun-

dently, who being much enraged, flung his club at Guy, with such force, that it beat him down; and before Guy could recover his fall Armarant had got up his club again. But in the end Guy killed this broad back dog, and released divers captives that had been in thrawldom a long time, some almost famished, and others ready to expire under various tortures. They returned Guy thanks for their happy deliverance ; after which he gave up the castle and keys to the old man and his fifteen sons.

Guy pursued his intended journey, and coming to a grave, he took up a worm-

eaten Skull, which he thus addressed, —
Perhaps thou wert a Prince, or a mighty Monarch, a King, a Duke, or a Lord ! —

But the King and the Beggar muſt all return to the earth; and therefore man had need to remember his dying hour. Perhaps thou mighteſt have been a Queen or a Dntcheſs, or a Lady varniſhed with much beauty; but now thou art worms-meat, lying in the grave, the Sepolchre of all creatures.

While Guy was in this repenting ſoli-tude, fair Phillis, like a mourning wi-dow, cloathed herſelf in ſable attire, and vowed chaſtity in the abſence of her be-loved huſband. Her whole delight was in divine meditations and heavenly con-ſolations, praying for the welfare of her beloved Lord, fearing ſome ſavage mon-ſter had devoured him.——Thus Phillis ſpent the remainder of her life in ſorrow for her dear Lord; and to ſhew her hu-mility, ſhe ſold her Jewels and coſtly robes, with which ſhe uſed to grace King Athelſtone's court, and gave the money freely to the poor; ſhe relieved the lame and the blind, the widow and the father-leſs, and all thoſe that came to ask alms; building a large hoſpital for aged and ſick people, that they may be comforted in their ſickneſs and weak condition. And according to this rule she laid up treasure in heaven, which will be paid again with life everlasting.

Mean time Guy travelled through many lands and nations; at last in his Journey he met the Earl of Terry, who had been exiled from his territories by a merciless traytor. Guy bid him not be dismayed, and promised to venture his life for his restoration. The Earl thanked Guy most courteously, and they travelled together against Terry's enemy. Guy challenged him into the field, and there slew him hand to hand, and restored the Earl to his lands.

The Earl begged to know the name of his champion, but Guy insisted to remain in secret, neither would he take any gratuity for his services.

Thus was the noble Guy successful in all his actions, and finding his head crowned with silver hairs, after many years travel, he resolved to lay his aged body in his native country, and therefore returning from the Holy Land, he came to England, where he found the nation in great distress, the Danes having invaded the land, burning cities and towns, plundering the country, and killing men, women, and children; insomuch that King Athelstone was forced to take refuge in his invincible city of Winchester.

C H A P. VI.

Guy fights with the Giant Colborn, and having overcome him, discovers himself to the King, then to his Wife, and Dies in her Arms.

THE Danes having intelligence of King Athelstone's retreat to Winchester, drew all their forces hither, and seeing there was no way to win the city, they sent a summons to King Athelstone, desiring that an Englishman might combat with a Dane, and that side to lose the whole whose champion was defeated.

On this mighty Colborn singled himself from the Danes, and entered upon Morn Hill, near Winchester, breathing venomous words, calling the English cowardly dogs, that he would make their carcasses food for ravens.—What mighty boasting said he, hath there been in the foreign nations, of thefe Englifh cowards as if they had done deeds of wonder, who now like foxes hide their heads.

Guy hearing proud Colborn, could no longer forbear, but went immediately to the King, and on his kneee begged a combat; the King liking the courage of the pilgrim, bid him go and profper. Guy walking out of the North-gate to Mornhill, where Colborn the Danifh champion was. —— When Colborn efpied Guy he difdained him, faying, Art thou the beft champion England can afford? Quoth Guy it is unbecoming a profeffed champion to rail, my fword fhall be my orator. No longer they ftood to parley, but with great courage fought moft manfully, but Guy was fo nimble, that in vain Colborn ftruck for every blow fell upon the ground. Guy ftill laid about him like a dragon which gave great encouragement to the Engiifh; but Colborn in the end growing faint, Guy brought the Giant to the ground; upon which the Englifh all fhouted with fo much Joy, that peals of ecchoes rung in the air.——After this battle the Danes retired back again to their own country.

King Athelſtone ſent for this champion
to honour him : but Guy refuſed honours, ſaying, My Liege, I am a mortal
man, and have ſet the vain world at
defiance. But at the King's earneſt re-
queſt, on promiſe of concealment, Guy
diſcovered himſelf to him, which rejoic-
ed his heart, and he embraced his worthy champion ; but Guy took leave of
his ſovereign, and went into the fields,
where he made him a cave, living very

penſive and ſolitary ; and finding his hour
draw nigh, he ſent a meſſenger to Phillis,
at the ſight of which ſhe haſted to her
Lord, where with weeping joy they embraced each other.——Guy departed this
life in her tender arms, and was honour-
ably interred.

His widow grieving at his death, died fiften days after him.

Their E P I T A P H.

Under this mable there lies a pair,
Scarce such another in the world there are
Like him so valiant, or like her so fair.
His actions thro' the world have spread
  his fame,
And to the highest honours rais'd his name
For conjugal affection and chaste love,
She's only equal'd by the blest above.
Below they all perfections did possess,
And now enjoy consummate happiness.

F I N I S.

FAIRY STORIES.

Containing,

I. The Blue Beard and Florina.

III. The King of the Peacocks, and Rosetta.

Whereunto is added,

An excellent New S O N G, entitled,

The F A I R I E S Dance.

Printed and Sold in Aldermary Church-Yard, Bow Lane, London.

LEANDER;
Or, The BLUE BIRD
AND THE
Princeſs FLORINA.

IN former days lived a Prince, whoſe ſtrength and riches made him formidable to his neighbours, but whar was his greateſt comfort he had one of the moſt virtuous and beautifulleſt Princeſſes living ; but his happineſs ſoon ended, for in a ſhort time ſhe died.

There was deep ſorrow for ſo great a loſs, and the King in particular grieved ſo much that he was reduced almoſt to death's door.

The court fearing his death, uſed their beſt endeavours to comfort him ? but all in vain.

At laſt, a cunning diſſembling widow undertook to baniſh ʻrom his Majeſty this melancholy that brought him to death's door. She veiled herself, and as the King commended his deceased Queen, she did the same by her husband. And thus the subtle widow so lamented, that it moved the King to pity her, and to forget his own grief.

Having gone thus far, and being a very beautiful woman, she began to throw away her veil, and managed her part so dexterously, that the late Queens' memory was quite forgotten, and he took her to wife.

At the time of his second marriage each of them had only a daughter; the king's was called Florina, the pride of the whole earth; the Queen's was named Truitoine, despicable, deformed, and of a very ill temper.

The daughter was a Jewel with the mother, who called her Charming Truitoine; but perceiving the charms of the beauteous Florina had gained the affections of the whole kingdom, she was resolved to lessen her esteem with her father which she tried all possible means to bring about.

In short time news came of the arrival of a noble Prince, who was called, The Charming King.—The Queen hearing of it, thought this was the time to make her daughter Truitoine happy; so caused her to be decked with the richest ornaments, ordering all the fine silks and jewels of Florina to be locked up; so that she having nothing left but an old gown, hid herself when the Charming King came to his audience.

He was received by the Queen with great respect, who presented her daughter, of whom the King took little notice, desiring to see the Princess Florina. There she stands in yonder corner, replied the Queen.—The king immediately addressed the Princess in such passionate terms that the Queen could not conceal her resentment ; and she prevailed on the King to confine Forina as long as the Charming King stayed at court.

To render all things to her mind, she ordered the Charming King's attendants to say base things of Florina ; but he did not heed them, saying, These stories are certainly the contrivance of the Queen, and her ugly daughter Truitoine ; and that nothing could compleat his happiness, but the possession of his beautiful Florina.

When the Queen heard it, she vowed revenge ; and was ready to burst at the thoughts of his affection for Florina, and the next time that he enquired for her, the Queen told him with some warmth, that it was her husband's pleasure she should not be seen till her daughter was married.

At this answer the King with seeming indifference departed.

At length the Charming King, found means to converse in the night with his beloved Florina, from her window, and

after a little importunity, he prevailed on her to consent to escape with him, which they agreed should be put in execution the next night.

The malicious Queen being informed of this by her intendant Fairy, removed Florina to a distant part of the house, and dressed up Truitoine as like her as they could, and placed her at the window, to wait the coming of the Charming King at the place appointed.

The time being come, the Charming King got ready a chariot drawn by flying Frogs, and repairing to the castle he there found the Princess at the window. In a moment he took her in his arms, and having seated her in the chariot, asked her where she would have the marriage consumated? The counterfeit replied, if he thought fit, it might be at her Fairy Grandmother's. Be it so, said the King to his coursers, who soon arrived at the Fairy Castle.

When Truitoine had conferred with her godmother, and told her the artifices she used to bring over the King to her embraces, and desired her assistance in this so critical a juncture. It is to no purpose said Souffio, it is but labour-in-vain, Florina has got his heart already; however to satisfy you, I will try some experiments.

Away went Souffio with Truitoine to the King, who stood amazed at seeing his ugly enemy, instead of the beautiful Florina.

Sir, said the angry Fairy, marry my daughter whom you promised.—Not I, said the King, you may persuade me to

well, to marry a cinder wench. Charming King, said Souffio, be not too rash.—
I will respect you as a fairy, said the king, give me but my true Florina.—Am not I she, said Truitoine, whom you promised, and is not this ring a witness? ——— 'Tis all a cheat, said the King, so come my little frogs, let us be gone.——Stay, stay says Souffio, ask my leave first; so touching him with her finger, he was, as it were nailed down to the floor.—If you kill me, said he, I will never leave my Florina.

They kept him in this posture for six weeks, using all possible means to persuade him: but Souffio, knowing it impossible, once more said, Will you wed her or not? ——— I will not marry such a filthy brute, said the King, nor trouble myself with her. — She shall not trouble you, said Souffio; but for breaking your oath you shall be a Blue Bird for seven years. — With that she opened the window, saying, You may take your flight Master Blue Bird.

She no sooner said it, but he immediately found himself in the shape of a dove, with an ivory beak and a tuft of

feathers upon his head; so stretching his
wings, he left the castle in an instant.

The Charming Knight, who fled some
time among the myrtle and cyprus trees,
singing melancholy songs, flew at length

where Florina lay: but as he would not
be discovered by Truitoine, he sung only
in the night on a tall tree, whose boughs
reached her window.

In short, words cannot express the joys
passed between them. When they part-

ed, they thought it long before they met
again, and thus discoursed :

Tho' my dear thy fate is hard,
    And the pains I feel severe,
Torments which I ne'er deserv'd,
    Yet our happiness lies here ;

They're but th' Effect of Woman's
        rage,
    The cruel Queen and Truitoine ;
A conquest Love doth still presage,
    When thee and I shall be but one.

In spite of all their hellish spleen,
Thou shalt be King and I thy Queen.

The Queen over-hearing these words,
stamped with her foot, crying Treason !
the mean while Truitoine burst open the
door.

Florina, to save the Blue Bird, had
just time enough to let him fly as the
Queen approached.

                              T H E

✕✕✕✕✕✕✕✕✕✕✕✕✕✕✕✕

THE
King of the Peacocks
AND THE
Princeſs ROSETTA.

❀❀❀❀❀❀❀❀❀❀❀❀❀❀❀❀

WHEN the Empire of the Fairies
was governed by the Empreſs
Truſſio, there reigned a King and Queen,
who had two ſons and one daughter ; the
daughter was every way lovely, and as
ſhe grew up became the mother's darling.
This made them conſult the Fairies concerning her fortune. They all agreed,
That ſhe ſhould paſs many difficulties,
and at length arrive to laſting happineſs ;
and that her two brothers ſhould be con-
demned to death on her account.

The King no ſooner heard it, but he
was for deſtroying the daughter in the
cradle, to ſave his two ſons. The Queen
begged ſhe might be ſaved till the opi-

nion of a famous hermit might be had, who advifed the King to confine his daughter to perpetual imprifonment, and fo he did ; and that fhe might not fhorten her days fhe had the converfation of her parents. And thus fhe fpent her time, till her parents fickened and died. And then the young King and his brother went and fetched their fifter, to confult about her marrirge.

As they walked along, the Princefs's little green dog Fretillon, who had but one ear, fell a barking at a ftately Peacock The Princefs admiring its beauty, faid fhe would take it to court with her ; and afked the King what it was? — He anf-wered, a Peacock.—Say you fo, fays fhe, then I'll die a virgin if I cannot have the King of the Peacocks for my husband.— And where fhall we find his Peacock Ma-jefty, faid he ? — Nay, fee you to that fays fhe, I'll keep my word.

In vain they took many a ftep after the King of the Peacocks, till they arrived at the Locuft Land ; where they were told, the King they fought lived about a thoufand leagues fouthward from that country.

With this information they departed
for that kingdom, where were Peacocks
perching on every tree, Said the King
to his brother, If the King should prove
a Peacock! our sister will bring forth
Pea-Chickens instead of children.

But they found the city full of people,
all bedeck'd with peacocks feathers, and
met the King on a stately steed, with his
cloaths adorned with diamonds.

117

As soon as he saw them he demanded their business. They informed him, They had brought a picture of their sister, a Princess by birth, who had vowed to marry no one but himself; and with whom they would give one hundred ton of gold.

The King smitten with the picture, said, If she appeared like it, he would marry her; but that if upon her arrival, she proved otherwise, they should both be executed as cheats; and ordered a guard over them till her arrival.

Upon this dispatches were sent for the Princess. She no sooner heard it, but she sent for her Nobles, and committed unto their care the management of affairs of state.

Having packed up her portion, commended her Peacock to them, and only accompanied by her old nurse, her nurse's daughter, and her one ear'd dog, she embarked, and put to sea as joyful as a new-married bride.

While at sea, many times had her designing nurse enquired of the Captain when they should land. —— At last this wretch took the Captain aside, and told him, that if he would throw the Princess overboard, he should be rewarded with a ton of gold ; and that you may do it in safety, I will dress my daughter in her cloaths, and she shall be married to the King.

The persuasions of the nurse with the help of strong liquors, with which she plied him so closely, worked him to her turn, so that at the midnight watch they threw the innocent Princess, bed and all as she lay asleep, with her little dog by her, into the sea.

Happy was it for the Princess that her bed was made of Phenix feathers, which never sink. The Princess had not been long overboard before the waves awaked her dog, who seeing the fish swim about him, barked so loud as to awake his mistress.

Next day the vessel came to the land, where an hundred coaches waited for the landing of the Princess. Among the rest was her body coach, of an inestimable value, with a noble train of very beautiful virgins.

Thus preparations was made for the reception of Rosetta ; while the nurse

dreſſed her ugly daughter in the habit of
the Princeſs, and carried her aſhore; but
when the King's ſervants ſaw her, they
were in amaze. — What ſaid ſhe, is the
reaſon of theſe fellows ſtupidity? ſee
how the blockheads ſtand! fetch me
ſome refreſhments, or I will have you
all flayed alive.

This language ſtruck them all with
horror; ſo they carried the Boſs with her
mother, and the unmannerly ſailors to the
King's palace; but never were people
more hiſſed at, nay even the Peacocks
ſcreamed out againſt her as ſhe paſſed by
them.

By this time the King was told they
were entering his palace, and he ſaw the
ſham princeſs amongſt the crowd, who
much derided her.

The King at firſt thought this was oc-
caſioned by ſome outlandiſh beaſt, but
when he ſaw her he ſoon perceived his
error.

It is hard to imagine the ſurpriſe he was
in at the ſight of her. — Have they, ſaid
he, thus impoſed on me? — Well, they
ſhall die for it. — Immediately he ordered
the Mother, Daughter, and Captain to be

imprisoned; and that the two Princes, already in custody, should be thrown into a dungeon, until brought to execution.

The King and the Prince his brother, seeing themselves in danger, remonstrated to the King, that what they had affirmed was true; that threatening to put them to death was indiscretion; and that the eldest of them was a King, rich, and powerful as himself, whose subjects, by whom he was beloved, would make him repent his rashness.

The King hearing this would have set them at liberty; but was told he would be ridiculed by all despotick princes if he did not execute them according to his word.

Immediately gibbets were erected, but by the assistance of the Mufti judgment was respited for seven days, they assuring him, they should be able to convince his Majesty of the mistake.

Things thus carried on, the Princess Rosetta, who lay forty-eight hours floating between hope and despair, was near starved with hunger, and had surely died, had not her little dog dived and brought up her oysters, muscles, &c.——— Ah! said she, would I were under my former confinement. Better I had never seen a Peacock. Sure the King of the Peacocks has revenged himself on me for loving him.

Thus she lamented her fate, time and tide were so merciful as to throw her a-shore by an old fisherman's cottage. The dog jumped on dry land, and barked to make the old man hear; where to his surprise he found the Princess crying out for help. He saw by the rich bed she was of illustrious birth, and immediately drew her out.

He soon took her home with her little dog, and in some homely cloaths of his daughter's dressed her like a shepherdess. After she was warmed and fed, he asked the cause of his misfortunes. The old man hearing all with vast attention, was for informing the King of the Peacocks, and to fetch some dainties from his table, but she said, My little dog Fretillon will be of more service to us, if you will but hang a little basket round his neck.

The

The fisherman did as she said, and the Princess cried, Go fetch me something out of the best pot in the King's kitchen. Away ran Fretillon, and watching his opportunity, took away a dozen of quails, and brought them to his mistress. — She sent him again, and he brought citron-water, Naples biscuit and preserved fruit.

When the King of the Peacocks was to dine, the servants were at a loss for the provision; so that in a fright they told the King his dinner was taken away they knew not how.

Then they provided for his supper, but the little one ear'd dog carried it to his mistress; so the poor King fasting thus, grew starving, and was forced to go to bed supperless.

He suffered thus for three days, till his Mufti found out how the victuals was carried off, who following the dog to the cottage, told his Majesty.

Immediately messengers were dispatched, where they found them feeding upon the King's provisions, as hearty as if it had been their own.

They presently carried them with the dog to court. And the next day being the last Princess Rosetta's brothers were to live, the King ordered the prisoners to be brought into the hall to die together; but when the King saw the beauty of Rosetta, his heart sunk in him, knowing the picture to be like her. He stood silent for some time, till the old man with bended knee declared her the true Rosetta, whom the nurse committed to the waves.

The King declared his Queen, in the mean time her brothers, the nurse, the daughter, and the Captain were come in, when the Princess fell upon her brothers necks, and embraced them, whilst she wept for joy. The wicked nurse and her accomplices, seeing themselves discovered, surrendered, and fell upon their knees to implore mery.

The Prince would have slain them, had not the good-natured Princess forgiven them, and perswaded him to do the same. She endowed the old fisherman with an estate, made him Knight of the Order of the Dolphins, and Vice Admiral of the seas. As for the little dog he was had in great favour at court, lay always at the feet of the Queen's bed, had a table served him each day with the legs and wings of the daintiest birds, and took the right-hand of all the dogs of quality.

The next day they were married in the presence of her brothers, who returned home well satisfied ; and nothing but joy was seen and heard at the King of Peacocks being wedded to the Princess Rosetta, who lived togethr many years afterwards enjoying all the blessing they could wish.

The

The F A I R I E S Dance.

A New S O N G

COME, follow, follow me,
   Ye Fairy Elves be;
Which circle on the Green.
Come follow M A B your Queen.

Hand in hand let's dance around,
For this place is Fairy Ground.

When mortals are at reſt,
And ſnoring in their neſt;
Unheard and unſpy'd,
Thro' Key-holes we do glide,
Over tables, ſtools, and ſhelves,
We trip it with our Fairy Elves.

And if the houſe be foul,
With platter, diſh, or bowl,
Up ſtairs we nimbly creep,
And find the ſluts aſleep;
Then we pinch arms and thighs,
None eſcapes, nor none eſpies.

But if the houſe be ſwept,
And from uncleanneſs kept,
We praiſe the houſhold maid,
And ſurely ſhe is paid;
Since we do uſe before we go
To drop a teaſter in her ſhoe.

Upon a muſhroon's head,
Our table we do ſpread:
A corn of rye and wheat,
Is manchet that we eat:
Pearly drops of dew we drink,
In acorn ſhells fill'd to the brink.
The brains of nightingales,
The unctuous dew of ſnails,

Between two nut-shells strew'd,
Is meat that's easily chew'd;
And the heads of little mice,
Do make a feast that's wond'rous nice.

On tops of dewey grass,
So nimbly we do pass;
The young and tender stalk,
Ne'er bends when we do walk:
Yet in the morning may be seen,
Where we the night before have been.

The grashopper and the fly,
Serve for our minstrelly:
Grace said, we dine awhile;
And thus the time beguile;
And when the moon doth hide his head,
The glow-worm lights us home to bed.

F I N I S.

The Interesting Story

OF THE

CHILDREN IN THE WOOD,

AN

HISTORICAL BALLAD.

———

BANBURY:

Printed by J. G. Rusher.

CHILDREN IN THE WOOD.

Now ponder well, ye parents dear,
   The words which I shall write,
A dismal story you shall hear,
   In time brought forth to light.

A merchant of no small account,
   In England dwelt of late,
Who did in riches far surmount
   Most men of his estate.

Yet sickness came, and he must die,
   No help his life could save;
In anguish too his wife did lie,
   Death sent them to the grave.

No love between this pair was lost,
   For each was mild and kind;
Together they gave up the ghost,
   And left two babes behind.

The one a fine and pretty boy,
　Not passing six years old,
A girl the next, the mother's joy,
　And cast in beauty's mould.

The father left his little son,
　As it was made appear,
When at the age of twenty-one,
　Three hundred pounds a year.

And to his daughter, we are told,
　Six hundred pounds to pay,
In value full of English gold,
　Upon her wedding day.

But if these children chanced to die,
　As death might soon come on,
The uncle then (none can deny)
　Made all the wealth his own.

4

Pisarius call'd his brother near,
    As on his bed he lay:
Remember, oh! my brother dear,
    Remember what I say?

This life I quit, and to your care
    My little babes commend:
Their youth in hopeful virtue rear;
    Their guardian, uncle, friend.

Their parents both you must supply,
    They do not know their loss,
And when you see the tear-swoln eye,
    For pity be not cross:

'Tis in your power (now alone)
    Their greatest friend to be;
To give them, when we're dead & gone,
    Or bliss, or misery.

If you direct their steps aright,
  From God expect reward;
All actions are within His sight,
  Of which He takes regard.

With clay-cold lips the babes they kiss'd,
  And gave their last adieu!
A heart of stone would melt, I wist,
  So sad a scene to view.

With tears, Androgus did reply—
  Dear brother, do not fear;
Their ev'ry wish I will supply,
  And be their uncle dear.

God never prosper me nor mine,
  In whatsoe'er I have,
If e'er I hurt them with design,
  When you are in the grave!

The parents being dead and gone,
  The children home he takes,
And seems to soften all their moan,
  So much of them he makes:

But had not kept the little souls
  A twelvemonth and a day,
But in his breast a scheme there rolls
  To take their lives away.

He bargain'd with two ruffians strong,
   Who were of furious mood,
To take away these children young,
   And slay them in a wood.

Then gave it out both far and near,
   That he them both did send
To town for education there,
   To one who was their friend.

Away the little babes were sent,
   Rejoicing with much pride;
It gave them both no small content,
   On horseback for to ride:

They prate and prattle pleasantly,
   As they ride on the way,
To those who should their butchers be,
   And work their lives decay.

The pretty speeches which they said,
  Made one rogue's heart relent;
For though he undertook the deed,
  He sorely did repent.

The other still more hard of heart,
  Was not at all aggriev'd,
And vow'd that he would do his part,
  For what he had receiv'd.

The other wont thereto agree,
    Which caused no little strife;
To fight they go right suddenly,
    About the children's life.

And he that was in mildest mood,
    Did slay the other there,
Within an unfrequented wood,
    The babes did quake with fear.

He took the children by the hand,
    While tears were in their eyes;
And for a scheme which he had planned,
    He bid them make no noise:

Then two long miles he did them lead,
    Of hunger they complain;
Stay here, says he, I'll bring you bread,
    And soon be back again.

11

Then hand in hand they took their way,
   And wander'd up and down ;
But never more did they survey
   The man come from the town.

Their pretty lips with blackberries
   Were all besmear'd and dy'd,
And when the shades of night arose,
   They sat them down and cry'd.

These pretty babes thus wander'd long,
  Without the least relief,
The woods, the briers, and thorns among,
  Till death did end their grief.

These pretty babes from any man,
  No funeral rite receives;
But Robin Redbreast forms the plan,
  To cover them with leaves.

And now the heavy wrath of God
   Upon their uncle fell;
The furies haunt his curst abode,
   And peace bade him farewell.

His barns consum'd, his house was fired,
   His lands were barren made,
His cattle in the fields expired,
   And nothing with him staid.

His ships, which both were gone to sea,
  Were on their voyage lost,
And fate did order him to be
  With wants and sorrows crost.

His lands or sold or mortgag'd were,
  Ere seven years were past,
Attend, and you shall quickly hear
  How prosper'd guilt at last.

The fellow who did take in hand
   The children both to kill,
To die was judged by the land,
   For murder—by God's will.

The guilty secret in his breast
   He could no more contain:
So all the truth he then confess'd,
   To ease him of his pain.

The uncle did in prison die,
   Unpitied was his fate:
Ye guardians, warning take hereby,
   And never prove ingrate.

To helpless infants still be kind,
   And give to each his right;
For, if you do not, soon you'll find
   God will your deeds requite.

THE END.

The trees are now felling in Blackberry Wood,
Where the ruffians did leave both the babes without food.

Death and Burial

OF

COCK ROBIN.

FRONTISPIECE.

The fields provide me food, and show
   The goodness of the Lord:
But fruits of life and glory grow
   In thy most holy word.

AN ELEGY

ON THE

Death and Burial

OF

COCK ROBIN.

———

Ornamented with Cuts.

———

YORK:

Printed by J. Kendrew, 23, Colliergate.

COCK ROBIN.

———

WHO kill'd Cock Robin?
  I, says the Sparrow,
    With my bow and arrow,
And I kill'd Cock Robin.

This is the Sparrow,
With his bow and arrow.

Who saw him die?
  I, said the Fly,
  With my little eye,
And I saw him die.

This is the Fly,
  With his little eye.

6

Who caught his blood?
1, said the Fish,
With my little dish,
And I caught his blood.

This is the Fish,
That held the dish.

7

Who made his shroud?
I, said the Beetle,
With my little needle,
And I made his shroud.

This is the Beetle,
With his thread and needle.

Who shall dig the grave?
  I, said the Owl,
    With my spade and shov'l,
  And I'll dig his grave.

This is the Owl so brave,
That dug Cock Robin's grave.

9

Who will be the Parson?
I, said the Rook,
With my little book,
And I will be the Parson.

Here's parson Rook,
A reading his book.

10

Who will be the clerk?
  I, said the Lark,
    If 'tis not in the dark,
And I will be the clerk.

  Behold how the Lark,
  Says Amen, like a clerk.

Who'll carry him to the grave?
   I, said the Kite,
    If 'tis not in the night,
And I'll carry him to the grave.

Behold now the Kite,
How he takes his flight.

Who will carry the link,
  I, said the Linnet,
   I'll fetch it in a minute,
And I'll carry the link.

Here's the Linnet with a light
Altho' 'tis not night.

13

Who'll be the chief mourner?
  I, said the Dove,
  For I mourn for my love,
And I'll be the chief mourner.

Here's a pretty Dove,
That mourns for her love.

Who'll bear the pall?
  We, says the Wrens,
    Both the cock and the hen,
And we,ll bear the pall.

See the Wrens so small,
Who bore Cock Robin's pall.

Who'll sing a psalm?
I, says the Thrush,
As he sat in a bush,
And I'll sing a psalm.

Here's a fine Thrush,
Singing psalms in a bush.

16

Who'll toll the bell?
  I, says the Bull,
    Because I can pull,
So Cock Robin farewell.

All the birds in the air,
  Fell a sighing and sobbing,
When they heard the bell toll
  For poor Cock Robin.

A PEEP AT THE

VARIOUS

NATIONS OF THE WORLD;

WITH

A CONCISE DESCRIPTION

OF THE

INHABITANTS.

Embellished with several neat Engravings.

NEW-YORK:

PRINTED AND PUBLISHED BY

S. KING, No. 148 FULTON-STREET.

*Of whom may be had the greatest variety of Toy Books and
Juvenile Pieces in the United States*

Recollections of Infancy.

A PEEP AT THE

VARIOUS

NATIONS OF THE WORLD;

WITH

A CONCISE DESCRIPTION

OF THE

INHABITANTS.

Embellished with several neat Engravings.

NEW-YORK:

PRINTED AND PUBLISHED BY
S. KING, No. 148 FULTON-STREET.
*Of whom may be had the greatest variety of Toy Books and
Christmas Pieces in the United States.*

ARABIAN.

ARABIA is a dreary country; more than half of it is a trackless level of sand, without shade or shelter, and scorched by the direct and intense rays of the burning sun; the higher lands, however, are more pleasantly situated, abounding in every thing that can add to the comfort or even luxury of the human race. Mecca, the place where Mahomet was born, and Medina, where he was buried, are the principal towns. Mount Sanai, and Mount Horeb, so often mentioned in Scripture, are also in this part of the world.

The wandering Arabs, are those who subsist on plunder, and infest the more desert parts; they have no home, living in tents, and move from place to place, as occasion or necessity prompt.

The Arabians are little known, as such, in his-

1*

tory; but they are far more celebrated under the name of Saracens; particularly in the history of the Holy Wars, which were carried on for so many years by all the Christian nations, for the recovery of Jerusalem, and which they, for a time, rescued, but were eventually obliged to abandon.

BOHEMIAN.

BOHEMIA, or Hungary, is a large tract of country, between Austria and Turkey, and situate about one thousand miles eastward from London. It is a very fertile country, and produces the finest ~apes grown in Europe.

The Bohemians are a hardy, active, and spirited kind of people; but much addicted to plunder: their forests, which are large and numerous, abounding with banditti

CHINESE.

CHINA is situated in the eastern part of the world, at about five thousand miles from London. It is an immense large country; being two thousand miles in length, and sixteen hundred in breadth. The land being surrounded with a high wall, thirty feet high, and so broad, that two carriages can, with ease, pass each other on the top.

Our tea comes from China, as do also silks, spices, and many other valuable articles of merchandize.

The Chinese are an indolent race of people, fond of shows and processions, and so much attached to their own country, that when once a man leaves it, he is never again allowed to return, being considered as unfit for their society, after mixing with the world. The women are most remarkable for the smallness of their feet.

The Chinese boast of an antiquity no other nation can or do pretend to. History, indeed, informs us that this empire was founded by Fohi, supposed to be the Noah of our Bible; but their traditions assert that they existed even long before the time at which we believe the sun or moon was created

DANE.

Denmark at present comprises eight islands, and a small tract of land, called Jutland. It is a flat country, abounding in bogs, and being surrounded by the sea, is subject to fogs and foul air. Little corn is grown here, and the pasturage is generally scarce; they subsist principally on fish, fresh and cured. The desolate and frozen regions of Greenland also belong to Denmark.

ENGLISHMAN.

ENGLAND, or at least that part of the United Kingdom, so called, is but a small island; and were it not for the ocean, which encircles its shores, instead of, being the most powerful nation in Europe, it would, long ere this, been merely a tributary colony of one of the continental states.

The English are a hardy, industrious, and uncommonly persevering race of people; and are celebrated in all parts of the world, for their enterprising spirit.

The United Empire of Great Britain comprises England, Ireland, Scotland, and Wales; besides immense possessions in the East and West Indies; indeed, in every part she has her colonies. Hanover, in Germany, is also subject to her control.

England has been several times overrun and conquered; the Romans, the Danes, the Saxons, the Picts, and the Normans, have, one after the other, been its masters;—its native inhabitants were mostly massacred; and if any trace now remains of them, it must be sought among the Welch; among whose mountains the persecuted Britons sought for safety from their invaders.

FRENCHMAN.

FRANCE is one of the finest countries in Europe. It abounds with every thing which can render life pleasant; its air is agreeable, and temperate, though rather warmer than England; and so healthy, particularly in the southern parts, that persons even in the last stage of a decline, have been restored to health, by a residence of a few months.

The French are a lively, agreeable people, much addicted to pleasure, and particularly partial to a military life.

France was, in ancient times, inhabited by the Gauls, a warlike, but barbarous race. It was conquered by the Romans twenty-five years before our Saviour was born; and again by the English in 1350; who held possession about one hundred years, when it was again re-taken by the French. Calais was the last possession of the English.

It is to France that the English are indebted for the advancement they have made in the silk manufacture. Louis XIV. to please one of the ladies of his Court, issued an Edict, or law, to exterminate the Protestants. In the dreadful confusion, thousands escaped, to whom protection and relief were afforded by the English nation; they settled in Spitalfields, where they established the silk manufacture.

GREENLANDER.

We have already noticed that this desolate country is under the dominion of Denmark; it is however of little consequence what prince claims it as his own, being a cold, inhospitable country, covered with snow during the greater part of the year, with a summer so short, as to render it uninhabitable to all but a few wandering tribes, who live in snow huts, and remove from place to place, as the weather gets warmer or colder.

Dogs are much used in these cold countries, in drawing the sledges: the men also walk in snow shoes, which prevent their sinking into the snow.

Greenland is the principal seat of our whale fisheries, and the place from which most of our oil and whalebone are brought.

The Greenlanders often venture out to sea in their little canoes, which are made of fish skin, and so light as to upset by a rough sea; but this accident has little effect upon the Greenlander, who, braced to his canoe, gives himself a sudden jerk, and soon rights himself.

NEGRO.

The western parts of Africa, are inhabited by a poor, unhappy race of men, called Negroes, who, to the eternal disgrace of Europeans, are bought and sold, like cattle. The other parts, however, are more civilized, and comprize several powerful nations. Egypt and Morocco are both in Africa.

2

HOLLANDER.

HOLLAND, formerly called the United Province, and now united into a kingdom called the Netherlands, consists of seven provinces, which are exceedingly well peopled, and make a considerable figure among the commercial nations of Europe.

The Hollanders are distinguished from other nations by their peculiar cleanliness, industry, and economy.

The whole of the United Provinces was formerly a swampy, marshy tract of uninhabitable land; but by industry and perseverance, the face of the country is entirely changed, and well-built towns, intersected with canals, and populous villages, are seen in every direction. Their houses and buildings are mostly erected on piles of wood driven deep into the earth.

The Dutch people are peculiarly excellent skaters. In the winter season, which in Holland is particularly severe, their canals, and even the entrances of their harbours, are frozen over, and covered with people skating in all directions; some with large burdens on their heads, some with the goods which they are taking to or from market, and even women with little childen in their arms, or fastened to their backs, are seen darting forward with the rapidity of lightning.

VENETIAN.

Venice is a beautiful and fruitful country, the fields abounding with vineyards and plantations of mulberries. Venice, the capital, is seated upon seventy islands, communicating with each other by canals, and by bridges of a particularly light and tasteful make.

ITALIAN.

ITALY, the remains of ancient Rome, and subsequently divided into twelve separate states, or governments, is an extremely beautiful country, and deservedly styled the Garden of Europe.

But beautiful as this large country certainly is, and so fertile as scarcely to require cultivation, to produce every requisite for the wants or gratification of mankind, yet the common people are wretched beyond expression; and thousands of beggars, called *lazzaroni*, infest the streets, to the no small annoyance and disgust of strangers.

The Italians are a revengeful race, and particularly attached to processions, feasts, and large parties.

In Italy, are two remarkable burning mountains; Mount Vesuvius, in Naples, and Mount Etna, in

Sicily; these dreadful places often burst out, and throw up vast quantities of hot cinders, stones, and dust: at the same time rivers of burning lava, or melted matter, rush down the sides, and urging forward, overwhelm the surrounding country for many miles. Two large towns, overwhelmed by an eruption which took place 1800 years ago, have been discovered, and exhibit one of the most singular, though awful instances of the instability of human power and greatness.

LAPLANDER.

LAPLAND, like Greenland, is, during nine months of the year, one mass of ice and snow, and for six months of the time, in total darkness. This dreary time is passed by the natives in caves dug in the earth, from which all cold is carefully excluded.

2*

OTAHEITEAN.

OTAHEITE is one of the South Sea Islands, discovered by Captain Cook, in one of his voyages round the world; the inhabitants are of a black hue, and particularly pleased with toys, such as looking-glasses, beads, and the like, and willingly part with their provisions in exchange. The Sandwich Islands are also in the South Seas.

RUSSIAN.

———

Russia, originally called Muscovy, and then but an insignificant, barbarous race of people, is now one of the largest, and promises soon to become, the most powerful, nation in Europe.

The Russians are a particularly hardy race, capable of great exertion, but much attached to festivals and merry makings.

PRUSSIAN.

—

PRUSSIA wars originally a dukedom, tributary to Poland; but in 1656, it was declared independent, and in 1701, created into a kingdom, under Frederic, their first king.

The Prussians were originally an idolatrous and cruel people; but since their elevation, they have become more civilized, and at the present day hold a respectable rank among the nations of Europe.

SWEDE.

SWEDEN, Norway, and Denmark, were in ancient time one kingdom ; but now Sweden and Norway form an independent state.

Sweden has neither spring nor autumn ; the summer, which lasts but three months, comes so quick upon them, that vegetation shows itself in a few days, and comes to perfection in a few weeks.

TARTAR.

TARTARY is a large tract of country, extending from China in Asia, to the confines of the Russian Empire in Europe. It is mostly inhabited by wandering tribes, although here and there a more settled nation may be found.

The Tartars are particularly partial to horses, and are, perhaps, the most expert horsemen in the world.

ZEALANDER.

ZEALAND is situated on the Northern part of America, and is inhabited by wandering tribes of wild Indians, who subsist principally by fishing and hunting. They worship the Great Spirit, as they call their Deity, because he is good; and they sacrifice to the Evil Spirit, as they call the Devil, because they imagine he will not then hurt them.

184

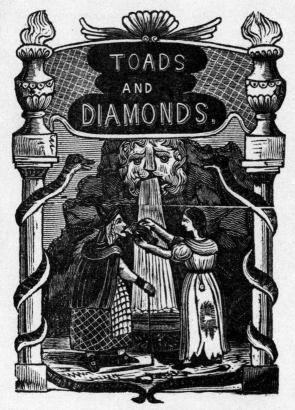

TOADS
AND
DIAMONDS.

J. Catnach, Printer, Monmouth Court, Seven Dials.

TOADS AND DIAMONDS.

There was, once upon a time, a widow who had two daughters. The eldest was so much like her, both in features and temper, that whoever looked upon the daughter, saw the mother. They were both so disagreeable and so proud, that there was no living with them. The youngest, who resembled her father in courtesy and sweetness of temper, was also one of the most beautiful girls ever seen. As people naturally love their own likeness, the mother doted on the eldest daughter, and at the same time had such an aversion for the youngest, that she made her eat in the kitchen, and work continually.

Among other things, this poor child was forced twice a day to draw water, above a mile and a half from the house, and bring home a pitcher full of it. One day as she was at the fountain, there came to her a poor woman, who begged of her to let her drink; "O, yes, with all my heart, Goody ;" said this pretty little girl, and washing out the pitcher, she took up some water from the clearest place in the fountain, and gave it to her, holding up the pitcher all the while, that she might drink the easier.

The fairy (for such she was, who had assumed the form of a poor country woman, to see how far the civility and good manners of this pretty girl would go) had no sooner drunk than she said, " You are so pretty, so mannerly, and so good, my dear, that I cannot help bestowing a gift upon you, and I now promise you that whenever you speak a word, there shall come out of your mouth either a flower or a jewel."

When this pretty girl returned home, her mother scolded her for staying so long at the fountain ; " I beg your pardon, mamma," said the poor girl, "for not making more haste," and in speaking these words there came out

of her mouth, two roses, and four
pearls, and four diamonds; "What is
it I see there?" said her mother, quite
astonished; "I think I see pearls and
diamonds come out of the girl's mouth!
how happens this, child?" This was

the first time she had ever called her
child.

The artless girl told her frankly all
that had passed, not without dropping
out great numbers of diamonds. "In
good faith," cried the mother, "I must
send my child thither. Come hither,

Jenny, look what comes out of your
sister's mouth when she speaks! would
not you be glad, my dear, to have the
same gift bestowed on you? you have
nothing to do but to go and draw water
out of the fountain, and when a certain
poor woman asks you to let her drink,
give it her very civilly." "It would
be a very fine sight, indeed," said this
ill-bred minx, "to see me draw water!"
"You shall go, hussy," said the mother,
"and go this minute." So away she
went, taking with her the best silver
tankard in the house, but grumbling all
the way.

She had no sooner arrived at the
fountain, than she saw, coming out of
the wood, a lady most superbly dressed,
who came up to her and asked to drink.
This, you must know, was the same
fairy who appeared to her sister, but
now assumed the dress of a princess, to
see how far this girl's rudeness would

go. "Am I come hither," said the proud saucy slut, "to serve you with water, pray? I suppose the silver tankard was brought purely for your ladyship, was it? however, you may drink out of it if you choose."

"You are not very mannerly," answered the fairy, without putting herself in a passion; "well, then, since you have so little breeding, and are so disobliging, every word you speak out of your mouth shall come a snake or a toad."

When she came home, and attempted to speak, she threw up a viper and a toad. The mother blamed this to her younger daughter, and ran to beat her, but the poor girl ran away and hid herself in the forest,

The King's son met her as he returned from hunting, and asked her why she was crying? when she told him that her mother ill-used her, and she was obliged to seek shelter from her cruelty. The King's son seeing so many diamonds and pearls come out of her mouth when she spoke, thought

that such a gift was better than any marriage portion in another, led her to the palace, and married her.

The sister made herself so much hated, that her mother turned her out, and she died in the wood.

J. Catnach, Printer, 2 & 3, Monmouth-Court, 7 Dials.

THE FOLLOWING LARGE

HALFPENNY BOOKS

JUST PUBLISHED BY J. CATNACH :—

Child's Guide.
Good Child's Book.
Jack and the Bean Stalk.
Tom Thumb.
Butterfly's Funeral.
Old Mother Hubbard.
Little Red Riding-Hood.
Puss in Boots.
Blue Beard.

Forty Thieves.
Children in the Wood.
Little King Pipping.
Whittington and his Cat.
Jack the Giant-killer.
Robinson Crusoe.
Crazy Jane.
Toads and Diamond.

SEVERAL OTHERS IN PREPARATION.

Catnach, Printer.

HOULSTON'S
JUVENILE TRACTS.

FOR THE AMUSEMENT AND IMPROVEMENT OF
YOUNG PERSONS.

No. 10.
THE ROD.

･･➤･◦●◐●◦･◂･･

LONDON:
PRINTED FOR HOULSTON AND CO.
65, Paternoster-Row.

Price One Penny.

THE ROD.

IT was on a Christmas evening, that Mrs. Rowland was sitting in the arm-chair, by the fire-side, with half a dozen little girls seated beside her, all as neat, and as clean, and as happy as children could be. I need not tell you the names of the children, nor describe the manner

in which they were dressed; they were good children, and that is a matter of much more importance than either their names or their dress.

Mrs. Rowland took the lead at the village Sunday-school: she had for some years devoted much of her time to such of the young people as attended the school, in the hope of being useful to them. The great advantage of having pious parents had been enjoyed by her, and she had been taught from her youth, to fear the Lord, and to walk in those paths of humility, usefulness, and obedience, which will ever prove paths of pleasantness and peace to all them who walk therein. She had not been without her trials, but they had been so far sanctified as to draw her nearer to God, and to make her more anxious to spread the kingdom of the Redeemer on earth, especially in teaching the poor children of the village to read the Holy Scriptures, in seeking to convince them that they were sinners, and in directing their youthful minds to that "Lamb of God that taketh away the sins of the world."

The children were, as I said, seated beside her, and she, in her customary kind manner, was talking with them, and endeavouring to make some profitable impression on their minds. Among other things, she spoke of the correction which children occasionally required, and her remarks are here given, under the hope that other young people may profit by them, besides those to whom they were addressed.

"Few things," said she, "are more difficult than to convince young people that the chastisement they receive is for their good. Every child looks upon the rod as a very unnecessary thing, and considers

K 3

the parent, or the schoolmaster, or the schoolmistress, who uses it, very cruel. Children imagine that when they grow older they shall be happier, because, then, they will not be in fear of the rod; but they are mistaken. There is a rod for every age, from the child of a year old, to the man of fourscore."

The children here looked at each other, for they had never heard before of a grown person having the rod, and that a man when he was fourscore years of age, should have it, was a thing quite beyond their comprehension. Mrs. Rowland, however, went on.

"What I have said may appear strange to you, but it is as true as it is strange, and I hope to make it as plain to your comprehension as it is to mine. By and by, when you are arrived at years of maturity, you will see the advantages you have derived from the rod. Now, by a rod, I do not mean a bundle of birch twigs tied up together with a piece of packstring only, but every chastisement which is inflicted on account of transgression. When the word rod occurs in Scripture, it frequently signifies chastisement. Thus, when the coming of our Saviour is foretold by the prophet Isaiah, it is said, 'He shall smite the earth with the rod of his mouth.' Now this could not mean a birch rod, but the reproof, the chastisement, with which he would visit the sins of the transgressor. And in the prophecy of the prophet Micah it is written—'Hear ye the rod, and who hath appointed it.' Now, a birch rod is made to be felt, and not to be heard; therefore the rod, in this case, meant the warning, admonitions, and chastisements of the Almighty, which ought ever to cry aloud to the conscience of every evil doer."

The children, who, before, whenever they thought of a rod, had always thought of a bundle of birch, a form to stand on, and a cap to be placed on the head, now understood, very clearly, that the word rod might with propriety be used to signify punishment for an evil deed. When Mrs. Rowland saw that she had made herself understood, she went on thus.

"I said, that there is a rod for every age, for the old man as well as for the young child, and it is, indeed, so necessary, that we cannot do without it. You very seldom hear of a child touching a red hot poker more than once in the course of his life, because the punishment follows the transgression so suddenly, and so sharply, that he is deterred from ever again committing the same offence. Now the birch rod acts in the same manner, and the tingling admonition it bestows makes a child afraid of repeating the offence. It was a saying of Solomon, the wisest of men—'He that spareth his rod, hateth his son; but he that loveth him, chasteneth him betimes.' You all know that a child spoiled by in-

dulgence is a plague to all who have to do with him. Foolishness and bad passions are bound in the heart of a child, and unless they are corrected and restrained, they grow stronger and stronger. If a boy and a girl were to be brought up without correction, they would be a reproach to their parents, and a burden to themselves.

"A child is punished with a birch rod, and a dunce's cap; and a boy who is older with a stick, or a whip; but when school-days are passed, there are rods in abundance for all sorts of errors. The trespasser is imprisoned; the thief is flogged, or transported; the highway robber is hanged; and the murderer is sometimes suspended on a gibbet, after he has died on the gallows. These rods are prepared by men to deter people from committing crime; but what I wish most of all to impress on your minds is, that God has prepared a rod for every sinner. He that sins must suffer, whether he be young or old, rich or poor.

"When a parent uses the rod, it is no proof that he does not love his offspring. He is afflicted in afflicting his child, but he does it for his good. In like manner, God uses the rod of affliction to make his people better. In his gracious promises to David, he says—'If his children forsake my law, and walk not in my judgments; if they break my statutes, and keep not my commandments; then will I visit their transgressions with the rod, and their iniquity with stripes. Nevertheless, my loving-kindness will I not utterly take from him, nor suffer my faithfulness to fail.' You see, then, that God loves his people, even when he chastises them; but if they will sin, they must also sorrow.

"A parent uses the rod according to the offence. If the crime be great, the punish-

ment must be severe. And God acts in the same manner with the disobedient. O how much punishment it sometimes takes to wean us from our sins! Three-fourths of all the sorrows which we experience we bring upon ourselves. If one affliction will not do, God is pleased to send another; if that does not succeed, a sharper rod is prepared, and a heavier burden placed upon us, till we cry out, and are glad to be delivered.

"Look at the rods which are endured by the determined enemies of God.—When Pharaoh, king of Egypt, refused permission to the Children of Israel to go with Moses into the wilderness, God sent a plague upon him; and, because that did not alter his resolution, he sent another, and another, worse, and worse; until he permitted the people to depart: and when, after all, Pharaoh's heart was hardened to pursue the Children of Israel, God commanded the raging billows of the mighty deep to overwhelm him and his people.

"God can send a destroying rod, as well as a correcting rod, as many have found to their cost besides Pharaoh."

FINIS.

R. Clay, Printer, Bread-Street-Hill.

Bibliography

Bibliography

I GENERAL WORKS

Ashton, John.
Chap-Books of the Eighteenth Century. Chatto &
Windus, 1882.
Reprints of chapbooks, many of which were
printed by the Diceys. By far the fullest collection, with some useful notes and facsimile
illustrations.

Darton, F. J. Harvey.
*Children's Books in England: Five centuries of social
life*. Second edition with an introduction by
Kathleen Lines, Cambridge University Press,
1958.
A standard work. Chapter V, 'The Pedlar's
Pack: "The Running Stationers",' deals with
children's chapbooks.

Halliwell, James Orchard.
*A Catalogue of Chap-Books, Garlands and Popular
Histories in the possession of James Orchard Halliwell,
Esq*. Private circulation, 1849.
Halliwell's notes upon the chapbooks in his
collection are extremely informative.

Lane, William Coolidge.
Catalogue of English and American Chapbooks and

Broadside Ballads in Harvard College Library. Cambridge, Massachusetts, 1905. Harvard College Library Bibliographical Contributions No. 56.
Indispensable for serious study. There are 2,461 entries, and comprehensive indexing of subjects, titles, publishers, printers and booksellers.

Neuburg, Victor E.
Chapbooks: A Bibliography of references to English and American Chapbook Literature of the Eighteenth and Nineteenth Centuries. The Vine Press, 1964.
An attempt to provide a reliable bibliographical guide to the study of chapbooks. Although subsequent research has revealed its lack of completeness, this book nevertheless remains the only general guide to the subject, and contains full lists of printers and publishers of ephemeral literature.

Opie, Iona and Peter, *Editors*.
The Oxford Dictionary of Nursery Rhymes. Oxford, The Clarendon Press, 1951.
A splendid book. Unfortunately the bibliography is inadequate, but this does not detract from the value of this unique work of reference.

Vries, Leonard de, *Compiler*.
Flowers of Delight. Dobson, 1965.
Useful only for the facsimiles of chapbooks.

Weiss, Harry B.
A Book about Chapbooks. Trenton, New Jersey, Private circulation, 1942.

One hundred copies of this book, containing 143 pages with 71 illustrations, were printed. The chapter on chapbook printers includes much detailed information. It is somewhat scarce, but there is a copy in the Bodleian Library, Oxford.

Weiss, Harry B.
A Catalogue of the Chapbooks in the New York Public Library. New York, 1936.
Another indispensable reference work. It is particularly useful for early nineteenth-century chapbooks, and the notes are especially valuable.

II   CHAPBOOK SOURCES

(a) *Medieval Romance*

Besant, Walter and Rice, James.
Sir Richard Whittington, Lord Mayor of London. Chatto & Windus, 1902. First published in 1881.

Dickson, Arthur.
Valentine and Orson. New York, Columbia University Press, 1929.

Dunlop, J. C.
The History of Fiction. Longman, Hurst, Rees, Orme & Brown, 1814. 3 volumes.

Ellis, George.
Specimens of Early English Metrical Romances.
Revised by J. O. Halliwell, Bohn, 1848. An extremely useful book which was first published in 3 volumes in 1805.

Keightley, Thomas.
Tales and Popular Fictions. Whittaker, 1834.

Morley, Henry, *Editor*.
Early Prose Romances. Routledge, 1889.
Useful, but the text is not always reliable.

Spence, Lewis.
A Dictionary of Medieval Romance and Romance Writers. George Routledge & Sons, London, 1913. E. P. Dutton & Co., New York.

Ward, H. L.
A Catalogue of Romances in the Department of Manuscripts in the British Museum. Volume I, 1883.

(b) *Jest-Books and Ballads*

Furnivall, F. J.
Captain Cox, his Ballads and his Books. The Ballad Society, 1871.
An excellent account of Elizabethan popular literature.

Hazlitt, W. C., *Editor*.
Old English Jest-Books. New York, Franklin, 1964. 3 volumes.
A facsimile reprint of the edition first published in London, Henry Sotheran, 1864.

Herford, C. H.
Studies in the Literary Relations of England and Germany in the Sixteenth Century. Cambridge University Press, 1886.

Hindley, Charles, *Editor*.
The Life of Long Meg of Westminster. Reeves &
Turner, 1871.
This reprint contains two versions of the chapbook, and is of interest as it shows the continuing popularity of this tale. The first version of
'Long Meg' was probably the black-letter edition, which came out in 1582. There was corres-
pondence—reprinted by Hindley—concerning
the authenticity of Long Meg, in Volumes 2, 3
and 6 of *Notes and Queries* (1850–52).

Lindsay, J. L.
*Bibliotheca Lindesiana: Catalogue of a Collection of
English Ballads of the 17th and 18th Centuries*. New
York, Franklin, 1962. 2 volumes.
A facsimile reprint of the first edition consisting
of 100 copies, which was privately printed, 1890.

Oesterley, H., *Editor*.
Shakespeare's Jest-Book. J. R. Smith, 1866.

Ritson, Joseph.
*Robin Hood: A Collection of all the Ancient Poems,
Songs and Ballads now extant relating to that cele-
brated English Outlaw*. Printed for T. Egerton &
J. Johnson, 1795. 2 volumes.
There was a new edition in 1832, containing an
Appendix. See also J. M. Gutch's *Robin Hood*,
2 volumes, 1847. Both Ritson and Gutch were
later reprinted in cheap editions.

Rollins, Hyder E.
An Analytical Index to the Ballad Entries 1557–

1709 in the Registers of the Company of Stationers in London. Studies in Philology, Vol. 21, No. 1, 1924.

III PRINTERS, PUBLISHERS AND BOOKSELLERS

(a) *General*

Plomer, H. R.
A Dictionary of the Printers and Booksellers who were at work in England, Scotland and Ireland from 1668 to 1725. The Bibliographical Society, 1922.

Plomer, H. R. and others.
A Dictionary of the Printers and Booksellers who were at work in England, Scotland and Ireland from 1726 to 1775. The Bibliographical Society, 1932. There is also a useful list of printers and publishers of ballads in the 'Bibliotheca Lindesiana' (*supra*, II(b) Lindsay). See also the present writer, *Chapbooks; The Harvard Catalogue;* and *The Catalogue of Chapbooks in New York Public Library* (*supra*, I).

(b) *Banbury*

Cheney, John.
John Cheney and his Descendants, Printers in Banbury since 1767. Banbury, private circulation, 1936. No author is given, but this book was mainly written by John Cheney. It is a major contribution to our knowledge of provincial printing in the eighteenth and nineteenth centuries. The firm is still in existence in Banbury.

Pearson, Edwin.
Banbury Chapbooks. A. Reader, 1890.

(c) *The Catnachs*

Hindley, Charles.
The Catnach Press. Reeves & Turner, 1869.

Hindley, Charles.
The Life and Times of James Catnach. Reeves & Turner, 1878.

Hindley, Charles.
The History of the Catnach Press. Charles Hindley the younger, 1887.
Some of Hindley's books were issued in large paper editions and limited editions. Their bibliography is complicated, and I have not attempted to unravel the problems here.

(d) *Newcastle and Alnwick*

Welford, R.
Early Newcastle Typography, 1639–1800. Newcastle, 1906.

Isaac, Peter C. G.
William Davison of Alnwick, Pharmacist and Printer. Newcastle, private circulation, 1964. Typescript.

(e) *Nottinghamshire*

Cropper, Percy J.
The Nottinghamshire Printed Chap-Books with Notices of their Printers and Vendors. Nottingham, Frank Murray, 1892.
Only 85 copies of this book were printed.

(f) *York*

Davies, Robert.
A Memoir of the York Press. Nichols & Sons, 1868.

IV AMERICANA

Clark, J. C. L.
Notes on Chapman Whitcomb (Dartmouth, 1785), Eccentric Poet, and Publisher of Mrs. Rowlandson's 'Removes' and other Tracts. Lancaster, Massachusetts, 1911.
A 22 page reprint from the *Clinton Daily Item.*

Duncan, W. H.
Josiah Priest, Historian of the American Frontier: A Study and Bibliography. Worcester, Massachusetts. American Antiquarian Society, 1935.

Heartman, C. F.
Checklist of Printers in the United States, from Stephen Daye to the close of the War of Independence. New York. Heartman's Historical Series No. 9, 1915.

Narratives of Captivity among the Indians of North America. Chicago, The Newberry Library, 1912. Supplement 1, by Clara A. Smith, appeared in 1928.

Rosenbach, A. S. W.
Early American children's books. Portland, Maine, 1933. This catalogue of a private collection

includes bibliographical descriptions of chapbooks issued by such publishers as Mahlon Day and Solomon King. A reprint was published in 1966 by Kraus Reprint Corporation, New York.

Skeel, E. E. F.
Mason Locke Weems, His Work and Ways. Mrs. Roswell Skeel, Jnr., Seven Gates Farm, Vineyard Haven, Massachusetts. Private circulation, 1929. 3 volumes.

Weiss, Harry B.
American Chapbooks. Trenton, New Jersey, 1938. 100 copies were printed for private circulation.

Weiss, Harry B.
American Chapbooks, 1722–1842. The New York Public Library, 1945.

Weiss, Harry B.
Mahlon Day, an early New York Printer, Bookseller and Publisher of Children's Books. The New York Public Library, 1941.

Weiss, Harry B.
The Printers and Publishers of Children's Books in New York City, 1698–1830. The New York Public Library, 1948.

Weiss, Harry B.
Samuel Wood and Sons, early New York Publishers of Children's Books. The New York Public Library, 1942.

Weiss, Harry B.
Solomon King, early New York Bookseller and Publisher of Children's Books and Chapbooks. The New York Public Library, 1947.

Winslow, O. E.
American Broadside Verse Imprints of the 17th and 18th Centuries. New Haven, Yale University Press, 1930.
See also *supra,* I, Lane, Neuburg and Weiss.

V ARTICLES ON CHARACTERS IN CHILDREN'S CHAPBOOKS

Brown, A. C. L.
'The Source of a Guy of Warwick Chapbook', Journal of Germanic Philology, Vol. 3, 1901, pp. 14–23.
See also p. 10 footnote for details of Crane's *The Vogue of Guy of Warwick.*

Palgrave, Sir F.
'Antiquities of Nursery Literature', *Quarterly Review,* January, 1819.
Later reprinted in the author's *Collected Works.*

Weiss, Harry B.
American Editions of Sir Richard Whittington and His Cat. Bulletin of the New York Public Library, June, 1938.

Weiss, Harry B.
'The Autochthonal Tale of Jack the Giant-

Killer', *Scientific Monthly*, Vol. 28, February, 1929, pp. 126–133.

Weiss, Harry B.
Something about Simple Simon. Bulletin of the New York Public Library, June, 1940.
See also Clouston, W. A., *The Book of Noodles,* Elliot Stock, 1888.

Weiss, Harry B.
'Three Hundred Years of Tom Thumb', *Scientific Monthly,* Vol. 34, 1932, pp. 157–166.

Appendix

The British Museum

The National Collection contains many chapbooks and children's books. The following notes provide details of a representative selection of such publications from the eighteenth and nineteenth centuries.

EIGHTEENTH-CENTURY CHAPBOOKS

1. Three volumes of Dicey chapbooks.
   Press Mark 1079 i 13
                      i 14
                      i 15

2. A collection of thirteen titles, including some interesting provincial imprints from Wolverhampton and Manchester.
   Press Mark 1076 l 7

3. A collection of twenty-one chapbooks, including one with a Norris imprint.
   Press Mark 1076 l 3

4. Twenty-four chapbooks—mostly fairy tales.
   Press Mark 1076 l 1

5. A collection of fifteen chapbooks, printed in London and Newcastle.
   Press Mark 1076 l 24

NINETEENTH-CENTURY CHILDREN'S CHAPBOOKS

The H. M. Lyon Collection of Children's Chapbooks.
The little books are unbound, and show a wide variety of London and provincial imprints.
   Press Mark C.121 aa 5.

The Kendrew Collection.
A collection of the publications of J. Kendrew. Besides chapbooks, many of Kendrew's other publications are included in this collection, which is preserved in a large guard-book.
   Press Mark 1870 c. 2.

Index

No attempt has been made to index all the material in the Bibliography, but appropriate references have been included where items in the Bibliography support information in the main text.

226